"This is a deeply informed, fascinating account of the varying fortunes of C. S. Lewis's writings in America. Initial misunderstanding and mistrust give way to respect, and then to reverence, and ultimately to something not far from idolatry. Noll tells the tale vividly, and the responses from Johnson, Farney, and Black point out some vital implications of this history for Christians today. A welcome addition both to Lewis scholarship and contemporary Christian self-reflection."

Alan Jacobs, distinguished professor of humanities at the Honors College, Baylor University

"An invaluable assessment of Lewis's reception in the United States, offering important insights into both Lewis's significance and the distinctives of the American religious mind."

Alister McGrath, Oxford University

"Every time I start to think there is nothing more to say about Lewis, a new book comes out proving me wrong. Mark Noll's *C. S. Lewis in America* helpfully maps the progress of the Oxford don toward the dominant position he now enjoys as evangelicalism's favorite Brit. Noll and his respondents helpfully evaluate and nuance Lewis's reception here. A valuable contribution to Lewis studies."

Phil Tallon, associate professor of theology at Houston Christian University

"Interesting and informative. Mark Noll sheds light on the various ways American readers received Lewis's early works and, in so doing, illuminates the state of Christianity throughout the United States more generally during the period under examination. A fascinating snapshot and a cleverly oblique approach to the study of church history."

Michael Ward, University of Oxford, author of *After Humanity: A Guide to C.S. Lewis's* The Abolition of Man

"From elite, secular newspapers to denominational magazines, C. S. Lewis's writings commending the Christian faith had an enthusiastic reception in America. In this prophetic and timely book, preeminent historian Mark A. Noll has uncovered the secret of Lewis's success: he was deeply learned, theologically focused, and unusually creative. Noll himself brilliantly models how to embody these traits today."

Timothy Larsen, McManis Professor of Christian Thought at Wheaton College and author of *George MacDonald in the Age of Miracles*

"Mark Noll offers the definitive account of Lewis's reception in mid-twentieth-century America. He skillfully uses that story as a window on the overall state of Christianity in America during an era."

George Marsden, professor emeritus at the University of Notre Dame and author of *C. S. Lewis's* Mere Christianity: *A Biography*

"Mark Noll's *C. S. Lewis in America* gives evidence to the principle that the academic enterprise consists in seeing patterns and exceptions. Without generalizing, no body of knowledge can be passed on to others. And without accounting for exceptions, no generalization is honest. Noll has mastered the art of abstraction. With faithful respect for the particulars, he writes as Georges Seurat painted—he applies each researched point after point to the canvas of his manuscript. What emerges is a masterpiece, unambiguous. The picture is clear. Noll convinces. All who read this book will understand, with good reason, the American fascination with C. S. Lewis."

Jerry Root, author of *Splendour in the Dark: C. S. Lewis's* Dymer *in His Life and Work* and professor emeritus at Wheaton College

"One hundred years on, it's almost impossible for us to imagine a C. S. Lewis who was merely an Oxford professor. Mark Noll's story gives us a Lewis before he was famous."

Jason M. Baxter, Notre Dame, author of *The Medieval Mind of C. S. Lewis*

C. S. Lewis

IN
AMERICA

READINGS
AND RECEPTION,
1935-1947

MARK A. NOLL

WITH CONTRIBUTIONS FROM
KAREN J. JOHNSON,
KIRK D. FARNEY,
AND **AMY E. BLACK**

Academic
An imprint of InterVarsity Press
Downers Grove, Illinois

InterVarsity Press
P.O. Box 1400 | Downers Grove, IL 60515-1426
ivpress.com | email@ivpress.com

InterVarsity Press® is the publishing division of InterVarsity Christian Fellowship/USA®. For more information, visit intervarsity.org.

All Scripture quotations, unless otherwise indicated, are taken from The Holy Bible, New International Version®, NIV®. Copyright © 1973, 1978, 1984, 2011 by Biblica, Inc.™ Used by permission of Zondervan. All rights reserved worldwide. www.zondervan.com. The "NIV" and "New International Version" are trademarks registered in the United States Patent and Trademark Office by Biblica, Inc.™

Excerpt from "The Apologist's Evening Prayer" by C. S. Lewis are used with permission from the C.S. Lewis Company, © 1964, 2023 CS Lewis Pte Ltd.

Figure 3.5: *HIS Magazine*, February 1944. Used by permission of InterVarsity Christian Fellowship/USA.

The publisher cannot verify the accuracy or functionality of website URLs used in this book beyond the date of publication.

Cover design: David Fassett
Interior design: Jeanna Wiggins
Cover image: C. S. Lewis, ca. 1940. Used by permission of the Marion E. Wade Center, Wheaton College, Wheaton, IL.

ISBN 978-1-5140-0700-6 (print) | ISBN 978-1-5140-0701-3 (digital)

Printed in the United States of America ∞

Library of Congress Cataloging-in-Publication Data

Names: Noll, Mark A., 1946- author. | Johnson, Karen J., 1981- contributor.
  | Farney, Kirk D., contributor. | Black, Amy E., contributor.
Title: C. S. Lewis in America: readings and reception, 1935-1947 / Mark A.
  Noll; with contributions from Karen J. Johnson, Kirk D. Farney, and Amy
  E. Black.
Description: Downers Grove, IL: IVP Academic, 2023. | Includes
  bibliographical references and index.
Identifiers: LCCN 2023020231 (print) | LCCN 2023020232 (ebook) | ISBN
  9781514007006 (paperback) | ISBN 9781514007013 (ebook)
Subjects: LCSH: Lewis, C. S. (Clive Staples),
  1898-1963–Appreciation–America. | Religious literature–History and
  criticism. | United States–Religion–1901-1945.
Classification: LCC BX5199.L53 N65 2023 (print) | LCC BX5199.L53 (ebook)
  | DDC 823/.912–dc23/eng/20230523
LC record available at https://lccn.loc.gov/2023020231
LC ebook record available at https://lccn.loc.gov/2023020232

30   29   28   27   26   25   24   23 | 12   11   10   9   8   7   6   5   4   3   2   1

To

MAGGIE NOLL

and

THE MEMORY OF
CHRIS MITCHELL

CONTENTS

PREFACE

G. WALTER HANSEN

A DRAMATIC OCCURRENCE struck the United States with surprising force during World War II and in the years immediately before and after. Audiences who witnessed that unfolding episode were stunned. That unexpected event was the striking effect of books by a Belfast professor of medieval literature at Oxford University.

In this book, American historian Mark Noll documents the astounding impact of books by C. S. Lewis when they first appeared in the United States in the turbulent years of 1935–1947. His study yields two results: (1) portraits of the audiences that responded to C. S. Lewis, and (2) challenges to emulate C. S. Lewis in our own turbulent times.

His portraits of audiences responding to Lewis pose intriguing historical contrasts. In the Roman Catholic response (chapter one), consider how the pre–Vatican II church's unanimous, enthusiastic appreciation for the defense of objective, universal moral values articulated by Lewis differs from the division between Catholic liberals and conservatives in our day. In the wake of the 1960s sexual revolution and Pope John XXIII's call to *aggiornamento*, or "updating," of the church with the Second Vatican Council (1962–1965), conflicting, diverse Catholic perspectives generated tension and even animosity in the Catholic Church. While official (magisterial) teaching on the traditional creeds has not wavered, the splintering of the church can be seen today as inflammatory rhetoric over many moral issues causes rifts in Catholic parishes and families. You can hear the loss of the moral consensus in our day as Catholics disagree with Catholics regarding abortion rights and same-sex marriage. Just listen to the spectrum of positions held by US bishops, some of whom assert that a pro–abortion rights politician such as President Joseph Biden, a Roman Catholic, should not present himself for Communion.

The response of mainstream media (chapter two), from the first review in the *New York Times* (December 1935) to the appearance of Lewis on the cover of *Time* (September 1947), reveals the state of American culture seventy-five years ago. The popularity of Lewis in that era points to, in Noll's words, a "late Christian culture," in contrast to the post-Christian culture of our day. The decrease of Americans who identify as Christian and the increase of the nones, Americans who deny association with any faith tradition, provide evidence that the beliefs of Christianity are rejected or at least forgotten by an increasing number in our society. Of course, nones sing Christian hymns at funerals and weddings and advance arguments based on Christian ideas about human rights, but the Christian theology for those hymns and arguments is mostly forgotten.

The appreciation of Lewis's works by both mainline Protestants and, eventually, evangelicals (chapter three) shows us a common center in the American Protestant world in the 1940s, in contrast to the polarization between progressives and right-wing evangelicals in our day. In his preface to *Mere Christianity*, Lewis says, "It is at [the church's] centre, where her truest children dwell, that each communion is really closest to every other in spirit, if not in doctrine."[1] The appeal to dwell in the church's center seems to fall on deaf ears and hard hearts in our day.

---

[1]C. S. Lewis, *Mere Christianity* (New York: Macmillan Company, 1952), viii.

These significant contrasts between the time of the early reception of Lewis and our time might make you wonder about the relevance of C. S. Lewis for our day. What is the enduring value in the work of Lewis? Noll answers this question in his conclusion by pointing to qualities in Lewis's writing for us to emulate in our thought, life, and work. The following three phrases based on Lewis's work encapsulate Noll's challenges for us today.

LEARNING IN WAR-TIME

I am struck by the absence of direct, explicit commentary on breaking news by Lewis. Yet, he was writing during war time. How did he keep from being terrorized by the horror of war? We find out by reading his Evensong message, "Learning in War-Time," October 22, 1939, delivered to students and faculty at Oxford University. "The first enemy," he says, "is excitement—the tendency to think and feel about the war when we had intended to think about our work."[2] He calls his university colleagues back to their intellectual work, the work of the mind: "To be ignorant and simple now—not to be able to meet the enemies on their own ground—would be to throw down our weapons, and to betray our uneducated brethren who have, under God, no defense but us against intellectual attacks of the heathen. Good philosophers must exist, if for no other reason, because bad philosophy needs to be answered."[3]

According to Noll, the enduring value of Lewis's work is that he was "deeply learned." Lewis, he writes, had an "extensive reservoir of literary knowledge." A challenge for us today is to free ourselves from the panic of breaking news and pursue a life of learning that is "in its own small way, one of the appointed approaches to Divine reality and the Divine beauty."[4] Though few of us are called to a life of learning

---

[2] C. S. Lewis, "Learning in War-Time," in *The Weight of Glory* (New York: Macmillan Company, 1949), 51.
[3] Lewis, "Learning in War-Time," 50.
[4] Lewis, "Learning in War-Time," 54.

as professors and students in a university, all of us need to apply this challenge to keep our focus on the responsibilities of our own spheres of life and work in our turbulent times. When each of us pursues our God-given calling, the light of love and beauty of grace will overcome the darkness of vengeful hate and cruelty.

LIVING WITHIN THE TAO

Lewis saw clearly that the dominant philosophies of subjectivism and pragmatism were inadequate responses to the force of Nazism. He points to the Tao as the Way out of the darkness:

> The Chinese also speak of a great thing (the greatest thing) called the Tao. It is the reality beyond all predicates, the abyss that was before the Creator Himself. It is Nature, it is the Way, the Road. It is the Way in which the universe goes on, the Way in which things everlastingly emerge, stilly and tranquilly, into space and time. It is also the Way which every man should tread in imitation of that cosmic and supercosmic progression, conforming all activities to that great exemplar.[5]

. The only way to avoid the abolition of humanity is to live within the Tao, the framework of transcendent, universal norms of truth, justice, goodness, and beauty. The illustrations of the Tao that Lewis provides in the appendix to *The Abolition of Man* are drawn from a wide range of religious and philosophical sources. They give abundant evidence for the apostle Paul's claim that the moral law of God is written on the hearts of all humans (Rom 2:15). The universal moral law, the Tao, establishes a standard for all human behavior: "Only the *Tao* provides a common human law of action which can over-arch rulers and ruled alike."[6] Lewis's illustrations of the Tao show that the moral standard for speech in all times and places for all people forbids slander and

[5]C. S. Lewis, *The Abolition of Man* (New York: Macmillan Company, 1947), 11.
[6]Lewis, *Abolition*, 46.

PREFACE

false witness against neighbors and calls for words of love, truth, and grace.

In the most widespread Chinese translation of the Gospel of John, John 1:1 reads, "In the beginning was the *Tao*, and the *Tao* was with God and the *Tao* was God." This translation has generated controversy because of the potential confusion of Christian faith with what Tao means in the Chinese Taoist tradition. But if we see Tao as presented by Lewis to be the universal values in all human traditions, then we can affirm that Jesus is indeed the full embodiment of the Tao. Jesus says, "I am the way" (Jn 14:6). In Chinese, he is the Tao. The challenge for us today is to shine the light of the Tao—Beauty, Truth, Goodness, and Justice—to dispel the darkness of destructive, inhumane powers.

SITTING IN THE WHITE-HOT FURNACE
OF ESSENTIAL SPEECH

In the final chapter of Lewis's *That Hideous Strength*, the gods of other planets come to the house of Ransom. He speaks to them in the heavenly language. Then, in one of my favorite lines ever penned by Lewis, we read: "For Ransom, whose study had been for many years in the realm of words, it was heavenly pleasure. He found himself sitting within the very heart of language, in the white-hot furnace of essential speech." Ransom's heavenly pleasure was anticipated heavenly fulfillment for Lewis's own longing as one who loved words. In his work, he was sitting in the "white-hot furnace of essential speech," purifying and refining his language.

Noll demonstrates that American responses to Lewis during the war all applauded the exceptional clarity and humor in Lewis's writing. His language was accessible, purged of academic jargon and empty platitudes. Lewis wrote in the time of the big lie of Joseph Goebbels, Hitler's minister for public enlightenment and propaganda. Goebbels famously said, "A lie told once remains a lie, but a lie told a thousand times becomes the truth." In the "white-hot furnace of essential speech," Lewis burned up the big lies of Screwtape, the insidious lies of pride, sophisticated lies of academic skeptics, and the smooth lies of politicians. The challenge for us today is to burn away all toxic speech so that our words bear the beauty of truth and goodness.

THE KEN AND JEAN HANSEN LECTURESHIP

I was motivated to set up a lectureship in honor of my parents, Ken and Jean Hansen, at the Wade Center primarily because they loved Marion E. Wade. My father began working for Mr. Wade in 1946, the year I was born. He launched my father's career and mentored him in business. Often when I look at the picture of Marion Wade in the Wade Center, I give thanks to God for his beneficial influence in my family and in my life.

After Darlene and I were married in December 1967, the middle of my senior year at Wheaton College, we invited Marion and Lil Wade for dinner in our apartment. I wanted Darlene to get to know the best storyteller I've ever heard.

When Marion Wade passed through death into the Lord's presence on November 28, 1973, his last words to my father were, "Remember Joshua, Ken." As Joshua was the one who followed Moses to lead God's people, my father was the one who followed Marion Wade to lead the ServiceMaster Company.

After members of Marion Wade's family and friends at Service-Master set up a memorial fund in honor of Marion Wade at Wheaton College, my parents initiated the renaming of Clyde Kilby's collection of papers and books from the seven British authors—C. S. Lewis, J. R. R. Tolkien, Dorothy L. Sayers, George MacDonald, G. K. Chesterton, Charles Williams, and Owen Barfield—as the Marion E. Wade Collection.

I'm also motivated to name this lectureship after my parents because they loved the literature of these seven authors whose papers are now collected at the Wade Center.

While I was still in college, my father and mother took an evening course on Lewis and Tolkien with Dr. Kilby. The class was limited to nine students so that they could meet in Dr. Kilby's living room. Dr. Kilby's wife, Martha, served tea and cookies.

My parents were avid readers, collectors, and promoters of the books of the seven Wade authors, even hosting a book club in their living room led by Dr. Kilby. When they moved to Santa Barbara in 1977, they named their home Rivendell, after the beautiful house of the elf Lord Elrond, whose home served as a welcome haven to weary travelers as well as a cultural center for Middle-earth history and lore. Family and friends who stayed in their home know that their home fulfilled Tolkien's description of Rivendell:

> And so at last they all came to the Last Homely House, and found its doors flung wide. . . . [The] house was perfect whether you liked food, or sleep, or work, or story-telling, or singing, or just sitting and thinking best, or a pleasant mixture of them all. . . . Their clothes were mended as well as their bruises, their tempers and their hopes. . . . Their plans were improved with the best advice.[7]

Our family treasures many memories of our times at Rivendell, highlighted by storytelling. Our conversations often drew from images of the stories of Lewis, Tolkien, and the other authors. We had our own code language: "That was a terrible Bridge of Khazad-dûm experience." "That meeting felt like the Council of Elrond."

One cold February, Clyde and Martha Kilby escaped the deep freeze of Wheaton to thaw out and recover for two weeks at my parents' Rivendell home in Santa Barbara. As a thank-you note, Clyde Kilby dedicated his book *Images of Salvation in the Fiction of C. S. Lewis* to my parents. When my parents set up our family foundation in 1985, they named the foundation Rivendell Stewards' Trust.

---

[7]J. R. R. Tolkien, *The Hobbit* (London: Unwin Hyman, 1987), 50-51.

In many ways, they lived in and lived out the stories of the seven authors. It seems fitting and proper, therefore, to name this lectureship in honor of Ken and Jean Hansen.

ESCAPE FOR PRISONERS

The purpose of the Hansen Lectureship is to provide a way of escape for prisoners. J. R. R. Tolkien writes about the positive role of escape in literature:

> I have claimed that Escape is one of the main functions of fairy-stories, and since I do not disapprove of them, it is plain that I do not accept the tone of scorn or pity with which "Escape" is now so often used: a tone for which the uses of the word outside literary criticism give no warrant at all. In what the misusers of Escape are fond of calling Real Life, Escape is evidently as a rule very practical, and may even be heroic.[8]

Note that Tolkien is not talking about escap*ism* or an avoidance of reality but rather the idea of escape as a means of providing a new view of reality, the true, transcendent reality that is often screened from our view in this fallen world. He adds:

> Evidently we are faced by a misuse of words, and also by a confusion of thought. Why should a man be scorned, if, finding himself in prison, he tries to get out and go home? Or if, when he cannot do so, he thinks and talks about other topics than jailers and prison-walls? The world outside has not become less real because the prisoner cannot see it. In using Escape in this [derogatory] way the [literary] critics have chosen the wrong word, and, what is more, they are confusing, not always by sincere error, the Escape of the Prisoner with the Flight of the Deserter.[9]

---

[8]J. R. R. Tolkien, "On Fairy-Stories," in *Tales from the Perilous Realm* (Boston: Houghton Mifflin, 2008), 375.
[9]Tolkien, "On Fairy-Stories," 376.

I am not proposing that these lectures give us a way to escape from our responsibilities or ignore the needs of the world around us but rather that we explore the stories of the seven authors to escape from a distorted view of reality, from a sense of hopelessness, and to awaken us to the true hope of what God desires for us and promises to do for us.

C. S. Lewis offers a similar vision for the possibility that such literature could open our eyes to a new reality:

> We want to escape the illusions of perspective. . . . We want to see with other eyes, to imagine with other imaginations, to feel with other hearts, as well as with our own. . . .
>
> The man who is contented to be only himself, and therefore less a self, is in prison. My own eyes are not enough for me, I will see through those of others. . . .
>
> In reading great literature I become a thousand men yet remain myself. . . . Here as in worship, in love, in moral action, and in knowing, I transcend myself; and am never more myself than when I do.[10]

The purpose of the Hansen Lectureship is to explore the great literature of the seven Wade authors so that we can escape from the prison of our self-centeredness and narrow, parochial perspective in order to see with other eyes, feel with other hearts, and be equipped for practical deeds in real life.

As a result, we will learn new ways to experience and extend the fulfillment of our Lord's mission: "to proclaim freedom for the prisoners and recovery of sight for the blind, to set the oppressed free" (Lk 4:18 NIV).

---

[10]C. S. Lewis, *An Experiment in Criticism* (Cambridge: Cambridge University, 1965), 137, 140-41.

INTRODUCTION

MARK A. NOLL

IMAGINE THAT IN the 1930s and 1940s transatlantic air travel had been as routine as it is now. Imagine also that C. S. Lewis had journeyed to the United States to converse in person with those who were reading his books on this side of the Atlantic. Through 1942, it was only a small number of mostly academics and reviewers for the nation's newspapers of record. But after early 1943 and the American publication of *The Screwtape Letters*, that number grew rapidly and from every intellectual, religious, and cultural corner of the land. These readers in America included well-regarded literary scholars, theologians, historians, and philosophers; figures destined for renown, such as Thomas Merton and W. H. Auden; masters of the radio, such as Alister Cooke, who would later become a fixture on public television; reviewers for the *New York Times*, the *New York Herald Tribune*, the *Saturday Review*, and other well-positioned periodicals; and many Roman Catholics, many mainline Protestants, and a few—but only a few—fundamentalists and evangelicals.

In actual, as opposed to imagined, history, we know only a little about how Lewis responded to what his American readers wrote about his works.[1] Yet we know in detail how Americans from these various

---

[1]For some of those rare instances, see page 10n1, 25n31, 34n46, 56n3, 57n6, 81n44, 107n21, 113n30.

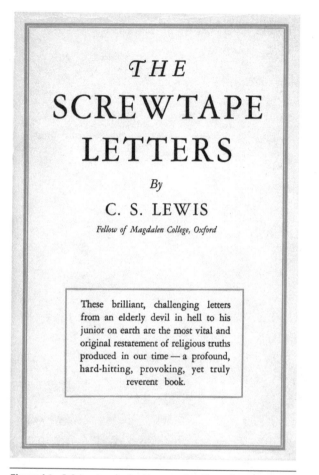

Figure I.1. C. S. Lewis, who had been noticed by only a small circle of academics, gained a widespread American readership almost immediately after Macmillan brought out an American edition of *The Screwtape Letters* in February 1943.

constituencies regarded his books because of the many reviews they published—at first a steady trickle and then, after *The Screwtape Letters*, a rapidly expanding deluge of critical engagement.

This book examines that engagement from before the *New York Times* published the first American review on December 8, 1935, through 1947, the year that *Time* magazine celebrated Lewis with a cover portrait and laudatory article in its September 8 issue. The logic for treating this span of years as a period unto itself is twofold.

For Lewis, these were the years when he first gained a significant audience in the United Kingdom and the United States. But they came *before* the stratospheric recognition that followed the publication in 1950 of the first Narnia tale (*The Lion, the Witch, and the Wardrobe*) and the appearance in 1952 of *Mere Christianity*, Lewis's apology and exposition of the Christian faith, which he assembled from pamphlets of radio talks he had delivered during the Second World War.[2]

The years 1935 through 1947 also mark a distinct period for showing what American critical reactions to Lewis reveal about Americans. This was an era dominated by pervasive national crises—first the Depression, then World War II, and then uncertainties after the war about charting a national course as the world's dominant superpower. These same years also witnessed a crucial cultural transition—from a past in which Christian values could be more or less taken for granted by wide swaths of the American people to a future in which those values became increasingly contested.[3]

In trying to make sense out of critical reactions to C. S. Lewis in the years surrounding the Second World War, this book follows outstanding recent studies by K. Alan Snyder, George Marsden, and Stephanie Derrick. By researching how, when, where, and why Lewis's writings became so popular, these books have greatly helped to understand the remarkable extent of the C. S. Lewis phenomenon.[4]

---

[2]Lewis's ongoing popularity is suggested by the fact that HarperOne leads a host of American publishers in keeping well over one hundred editions of over a dozen of his books in print. On Amazon.com's bestseller lists, various sets of the Narnia tales regularly rank in the top ten for "Children's Christian Faith Books," as do several versions of *Mere Christianity* (print, audio, and Kindle) in the top ten for "Christian Apologetics." The only Lewis work from before 1947 that ranks as high on these lists is *The Screwtape Letters*, which has long been a fixture at number one in "Christian Classics and Allegories."
[3]Awareness of that transition is discussed in the last part of chapter three.
[4]K. Alan Snyder, *America Discovers C. S. Lewis: His Profound Impact* (Eugene, OR: Wipf & Stock, 2016); George M. Marsden, *C. S. Lewis's* Mere Christianity: *A Biography* (Princeton,

Figure I.2. This image (ca. 1940) shows a considerably younger Lewis than the individual whom later photographs would make so well known throughout the whole world.

C. S. Lewis in America goes further by differentiating in considerable detail among the various American groups that responded to Lewis in the first years of his public visibility: first, the many Roman Catholics who wrote about Lewis and his works; second, Lewis's reception in journals, magazines, and newspapers intended for general audiences or the academic world; and third, responses to Lewis from

NJ: Princeton University Press, 2016); Stephanie L. Derrick, *The Fame of C. S. Lewis: A Controversialist's Reception in Britain and America* (New York: Oxford University Press, 2018).

Table 1. Publication of C. S. Lewis's Books in the United States, 1935–1947

TITLE	FIRST AMERICAN PUBLICATION	FIRST BRITISH PUBLICATION
Literary Scholarship		
The Allegory of Love	1958 (Oxford University Press, NY)	1936 (Clarendon)
Rehabilitations and Other Essays	1939, March 23 (Oxford University Press, London & New York)	
The Personal Heresy, with E. M. W. Tillyard	1939, April 27 (Oxford University Press, London & New York)	
A Preface to Paradise Lost	1942, October 8 (Oxford University Press, London & New York)	
as editor, George MacDonald: An Anthology	1947 (Macmillan)	1946 (Geoffrey Bles)
Imaginative Writing		
The Pilgrim's Regress	1935, October (Sheed & Ward)	1933 (J. M. Dent)
The Screwtape Letters	1943, February 16 (Macmillan)	1942, February 9 (Geoffrey Bles)
Out of the Silent Planet	1943, September 28 (Macmillan)	1938, September 23 (John Lane The Bodley Head)
Perelandra	1944, April 11 (Macmillan)	1943, April 20 (John Lane The Bodley Head)
The Great Divorce	1946, February 26 (Macmillan)	1946, January 14 (Geoffrey Bles/Centenary Press)
That Hideous Strength	1946, May 21 (Macmillan)	1945, August 16 (John Lane The Bodley Head)
Christian Exposition		
The Case for Christianity (US) / Broadcast Talks (UK)	1943, September 7 (Macmillan)	1942, July 13 (Geoffrey Bles/Centenary Press)
The Problem of Pain	1943, October 26 (Macmillan)	1940, October 18 (Centenary Press)
Christian Behaviour	1944, January 18 (Macmillan)	1943, April 19 (Geoffrey Bles/Cenenary Press)
Christian Exposition		
Beyond Personality: The Christian Idea of God	1945, March 20 (Macmillan)	1944, October 9 (Geoffrey Bles/Centenary Press)
The Abolition of Man	1947, April 8 (Macmillan)	1943, January 6 (Oxford University Press)
Miracles: A Preliminary Study	1947, September 16 (Macmillan)	1947, May 12 (Geoffrey Bles/Centenary Press)

Source: Walter Hooper, *C. S. Lewis: A Complete Guide to His Life and Works* (San Francisco: HarperSanFrancisco, 1996).

mainline Protestants and fundamentalist or evangelical Protestants. The chapter devoted to each group shows how the critical reception of C. S. Lewis sheds light on the history of that particular constituency in the years surrounding World War II. In other words, by bringing together what Lewis wrote and what Americans wrote about Lewis, we gain deeper insight into both Lewis and America.

Between 1935 and 1947, Americans enjoyed access to seventeen of Lewis's books. The Catholic firm Sheed & Ward published the first American edition of *The Pilgrim's Regress* in 1935. Soon four books from Lewis's literary scholarship became accessible through the New York office of Oxford University Press. Beginning in 1943, Macmillan was responsible for twelve titles, including two fantasies (*The Screwtape Letters* and *The Great Divorce*); the Ransom Trilogy (a.k.a. Space Trilogy); three slim volumes of radio presentations lectures that later became *Mere Christianity*; three works of Christian or moral argument (*The Problem of Pain*, *The Abolition of Man*, and *Miracles*); and Lewis's edited collection of writings from George MacDonald.

At the end of chapter three, *C. S. Lewis in America* draws to a close by considering matters of contemporary relevance. Documenting the reception of Lewis's writing during this early period underscores the enduring qualities that have kept these works alive for so many readers in so many places. Attending to this reception history may in turn suggest how the approaches Lewis modeled decades ago might assist believers in addressing the public today.

———————

This book, with a modest expansion and further editing, presents the lectures and responses that were first given at Wheaton College in early 2022 as the seventh series of the Ken and Jean Hansen Lectures at Wheaton's Marion E. Wade Center. In preparing the lectures for publication, I have retained some features of the original oral presentations while revising the chapters with a general readership in view.

At a time of increasing pressure on the humanities in colleges and universities, and indeed of resistance everywhere to careful intellectual labor, philanthropy as exemplified by Walter and Darlene Hansen in endowing a lectureship in honor of Walter's parents becomes all the more meaningful. It is thus an honor to thank both generations of Hansens for their long-standing commitment to the authors curated at the Wade Center, for making this lecture series possible, and for their overarching desire to show that Christian learning can be pursued as a God-given task.

I am also deeply grateful to Marjorie Mead of the Wade Center for organizing the lectures as well as to Crystal Downing, David Downing, Laura Schmidt, and other Wade staff for all that was involved in bringing off a lecture series in pandemic times. Chloe DuBois and Elise Peterson deserve special mention for their diligence in pursuit of the book's images. Jerry Root and Lyle Dorsett do not realize how greatly I benefited from the many hours of illuminating conversation in which they indulged me on matters relating to C. S. Lewis. A special word of thanks is due to Karen Johnson, Kirk Farney, and Amy Black for the care with which they prepared their responses to the lectures and the depth of insight those responses add to this book. For the images reproduced in the book, I would like to thank the owners of rights to those images. I am particularly grateful to *America* magazine for permission to reprint as an appendix to this volume the two pathbreaking articles on Lewis, authored by Charles Brady, that appeared in the May 27, 1944, and June 10, 1944, issues of that periodical.

C. S. Lewis in America is dedicated to my wife, Maggie Noll, and to a former director of the Wade Center, the late Chris Mitchell, and for very good reasons. Maggie undertook the research that led to a nearly complete collection of early American reviews of Lewis's works and then carefully organized that research while I was teaching at the University of Notre Dame. The project itself, however, came about only because Chris had asked me to prepare a talk as part of an observance in 2013 to mark the fiftieth anniversary of C. S. Lewis's death. It was a poignant but also joyful occasion in late 2021 to take part at the Wade Center in launching a book of essays in grateful memory of Chris, a book in which a preliminary essay based on Maggie's research was published.[5]

---

[5]Mark A. Noll, "C. S. Lewis in America, 1933–1943," in *The Undiscovered Lewis: Essays in Memory of Christopher W. Mitchell,* ed. Bruce D. Johnson (Hamden, CT: Winged Lion, 2021), 55-74. The book before you offers a different and much fuller consideration of the subject.

SURPRISE

ROMAN CATHOLICS AS LEWIS'S FIRST
AND MOST APPRECIATIVE READERS

MARK A. NOLL

FOR NEARLY EIGHTY YEARS, C. S. Lewis has sustained an incredible popularity in the United States. The beginning point of that popularity can be identified exactly. On February 16, 1943, the American publisher Macmillan brought out a New York edition of *The Screwtape Letters* a year after the book had been published in England. By the end of March, rapturous notices of the book had appeared in the *Atlanta Constitution*, the *Los Angeles Times*, the *Springfield Republican*, the *New York Times*, and the *Christian Century*. Sensing sales, Macmillan in October rushed into print two Lewis titles that had appeared earlier on the other side of the Atlantic, *Out of the Silent Planet* and *The Problem of Pain*. Immediately, American newspapers, magazines, and journals sprang to celebrate these works with almost as much enthusiasm as had greeted *Screwtape*.

Prominent in the initial chorus of praise for Lewis's work were positive reviews of *Screwtape* in *Commonweal*, a magazine published by lay Roman Catholics, and *America*, sponsored by the nation's Jesuits. *Thought*, a Catholic academic quarterly from Fordham University, had even jumped the gun in January with a sparkling review of the English edition.

This initial enthusiasm led to Catholic engagement that was remarkable in several respects. Catholic authors reviewed or discussed all seventeen of Lewis's books that could be read in America (see table 1). No other religious or academic constituency treated both popular and academic works so thoroughly. Beginning in early 1943, in what is still an incomplete accounting, American Catholics published at least thirty-four reviews and one extensive essay review in Catholic publications. They added five substantial reviews in the major New York newspapers. The high point in this wave of interest came in an extensive two-part essay in 1944 by Charles Brady, a professor of English literature at Canisius College, whom Lewis himself called "the first of my critics so far who has really read and understood *all* of my books and 'made up' the subject in a way that makes you an authority."[1] Although Catholic responses did include some negative criticism, they were more generally positive about Lewis than any other American constituency. Not until 1946, when Chad Walsh, an Episcopalian English professor at Beloit College, began to publish on Lewis did anyone else even come close to the breadth of Catholic treatment or the depth of Catholic appreciation.

To explore this episode in reception history, it helps to begin with a simplified account of the state of the church in the 1930s and 1940s. Then a survey of which Catholic authors highlighted which features of Lewis's writing will make it obvious why he was received so warmly. That survey, in turn, will put us in position not to claim that Lewis exerted the kind of influence on American Catholics that he would later exert on American evangelical Protestants but to show why Catholic responses to Lewis provide a telling gauge for crucially important developments that were underway in the American church.

---

[1]C. S. Lewis to Charles A. Brady, October 29, 1944, in *Books, Broadcasts, and the War, 1931–1949*, vol. 2 of *The Collected Letters of C. S. Lewis*, ed. Walter Hooper (San Francisco: HarperSanFrancisco, 2004), 629-31, quotation 629.

THE STATE OF THE CHURCH

Catholics themselves have made some of the harshest statements describing the American church of this era as isolated, ingrown, defensive, intellectually feeble, and dominated by an authority structure with practically no place for lay initiative or lay agency. William Cavanaugh, a distinguished scholar at DePaul University whose works have been much appreciated by evangelical Protestants, recently wrote about the insularity of his parents' church in the 1940s, which was "still running on the fumes of immigrant culture." In his account, "a Catholic of that generation was born in a Catholic hospital, was baptized and received weekly sacraments in a Catholic church, was educated in Catholic schools, attended bingo and smokers at the Catholic parish on weekends, and was buried in a Catholic cemetery. . . . Being Catholic was an identity expressed by cheering on the Notre Dame football team."[2]

William Shannon, the founding president of the Thomas Merton Society, introduced the fiftieth anniversary edition of Merton's hugely popular 1948 autobiography, *The Seven Storey Mountain*, with an even bleaker description of "the pre–Vatican II church into which Merton was baptized." (Merton's review in the *New York Times* of one of Lewis's early books is noted below.) According to Shannon, Merton brought a breath of fresh air into the American church, which was burdened with a straitjacketed theology "of prepackaged responses to any and all questions. Polemical and apologetic in tone, its aim was to prove that Catholics were right and all others wrong."[3]

In his magisterial account of Catholic higher education in the twentieth century, Philip Gleason explains that the dominance of medieval Neo-Scholasticism in the American church did have the

---

[2]William T. Cavanaugh, "The Church Among Idols: How My Mind Has Changed," *Christian Century*, June 16, 2021, 27, 31.

[3]William Shannon, "A Note to the Reader," in *The Seven Storey Mountain: An Autobiography of Faith*, by Thomas Merton (New York: Harcourt Brace, 1998), xx.

advantage of giving Catholic intellectual life a stable framework. But he adds that its often wooden presentation created difficulties because of "Catholics' near obsession with order and unity."[4] Karen Johnson's research on Catholic interracialism in Chicago during the middle decades of the century shows how difficult it was for laywomen and laymen to move the church to support racial justice. She quotes one priest of the era who, in a stereotypical view of the laity, claimed that their role was simply to "pay, pray, and obey."[5] Although these negative assessments about midcentury Catholicism are far from the whole story, they do reflect at least partial realities about a church whose increasing numbers, increasing wealth, and increasing educational attainments were only beginning to modify its insular and tradition-bound character.

Beyond these developments internal to the church, the years immediately after World War II witnessed an upsurge of American and especially American Protestant suspicion. Shortly before, as Catholics rallied with Protestants and also Jews to oppose European fascism, age-old antagonisms seemed to be relaxing. But soon thereafter, among other secular voices, Paul Blanshard of *The Nation* went on a rampage in a bestselling book that contrasted *American Freedom and Catholic Power* (1949), and respected Protestant ethicist Reinhold Niebuhr expressed similar fears privately, while White evangelicals used the recently founded National Association of Evangelicals to repeat traditional American Protestant fears about Catholic

---

[4]Philip Gleason, *Contending with Modernity: Catholic Higher Education in the Twentieth Century* (New York: Oxford University Press, 1995), 121.

[5]Karen J. Johnson, *One in Christ: Chicago Catholics and the Quest for Interracial Justice* (New York: Oxford University Press, 2018), 27. For a similar assessment, see Patrick Allitt, "The Forgotten Heritage of American Christian Socialism," *American Political Thought* 9 (Fall 2020): 631: "American Catholics in those days were mainly the children of immigrants from southern and eastern Europe or the descendants of immigrants from the Irish famine of the 1840s. Deferential to the clergy, the laity rarely took any initiative in religious matters. Their leaders, the princely midcentury bishops and cardinals, urged their flock to strive for middle-class respectability and worldly success while keeping the faith."

intolerance and despotism.[6] In a word, it is an exaggeration to say that the American Catholic Church in this era was feared, isolated, and ingrown. But it is not a complete exaggeration.

CATHOLIC LEWIS CRITICISM

Five Catholic periodicals, along with the *New York Times* and the *New York Herald Tribune*, supplied most of the Catholic Lewis criticism.[7] The nation's Jesuit community was responsible for *America*, a weekly magazine aimed at an educated general audience, as well as *Thought*, a quarterly published by Fordham University. Like *America*, *Commonweal* was a weekly edited by educated Catholics for educated Catholics but overseen by an independent lay board.[8] The Missionary Society of St. Paul the Apostle, or the Paulists, had been founded in the nineteenth century by Isaac Hecker with the goal of presenting a positive view of Catholicism to an American public shaped by Protestants' long-standing disdain for their faith. The Paulists published *The Catholic World*, a monthly targeting the same kind of general audience as *America* and *Commonweal*. Finally, the *American Ecclesiastical Review*, "a monthly publication for the clergy," sponsored by the Catholic University of America, was the one publication where Lewis's work was not well-received.

Before detailing the criticism, it is helpful to have a kind of scorecard overview of American Catholic assessments. Of Lewis's ten works that were noticed at least twice by Catholic authors, five received positive or even enthusiastically positive notices (with very

---

[6]See John T. McGreevy, *Catholicism and American Freedom: A History* (New York: Norton, 2003), 166-69 (Blanshard), 206, 211 (Niebuhr); Mark A. Noll and Carolyn Nystrom, *Is the Reformation Over? An Evangelical Assessment of Contemporary Roman Catholicism* (Grand Rapids: Baker, 2005), 37-40, 55-58; and William M. Shea, *The Lion and the Lamb: Evangelicals and Catholics in America* (New York: Oxford University Press, 2004), passim.

[7]Other notices appeared in *Our Sunday Visitor*, November 26, 1944; *Dominicana*, and *Theological Studies*.

[8]For its history, see "A Brief History of Commonweal," *Commonweal*, www.commonwealmagazine.org/about/history (accessed August 12, 2022).

occasional quibbles): *The Pilgrim's Regress, The Screwtape Letters, Perelandra, The Great Divorce,* and *The Abolition of Man.* Three works received mostly positive reviews: *Out of the Silent Planet, The Case for Christianity,* and *The Problem of Pain.* For two others, Catholic judgments were mixed: *Beyond Personality* and *That Hideous Strength.*

Although Catholic criticism was important for what it said about Lewis, for our purposes it was even more important for what it revealed about those who penned that criticism. From this angle, we find out *who* the authors were who interacted with the Oxford don, *whether* they were clerics or from the laity, *what* they highlighted for praise and occasional disagreement, and *how much* they referenced official Catholic teaching in making their judgments.

From first to last in this twelve-year period, the predominant note remained heartfelt appreciation. When in 1936 Father Bernard L. Conway, CSP, reviewed *The Pilgrim's Regress* in the Paulist's *Catholic World,* he could barely contain himself. Conway, the priest of the Church of the Paulist Fathers in New York City and a Catholic Defense Lecturer charged with responding to attacks on his church, hailed the allegory as a "brilliantly written volume" with "a devastating critique of modern philosophy, religion, politics, and art." The allegory, executed with "consummate skill," was "a clear-cut, logical and effective apologia of reason and the Christian faith." He concluded, "We have rarely read a book we so thoroughly enjoyed."[9]

A decade later, in 1946, two reviewers in *Dominicana,* identified only by their initials, praised two other titles almost as enthusiastically. This magazine described itself as "a publication of friars in formation at the Dominican House of Studies." About *That Hideous Strength,* the reviewers stated, "As always, Mr. Lewis' writing is brilliant." Yet they also wanted it understood that this fantasy was much

---

[9]B. L. C. [Bernard L. Conway], review of *The Pilgrim's Regress, The Catholic World* 143 (May 1936): 239-40.

more than merely entertaining, since its message, though "clothed in a symbolism," was "profound without ever becoming obscure." About *The Great Divorce*, the reviewers did warn that "caution must be exercised with regard to author Lewis' statements concerning the Catholic Doctrine of Purgatory and also the doctrine of Predestination." But these matters in "no way affect the over-all excellence of the book," which they called "a truly delightful presentation of a tremendous truth" that "consequently deserves a warm reception from the Catholic reading public."[10]

As the availability of Lewis's books increased, so also increased the chorus of praise, as when in late 1943 George Shuster published a strong commendation of *The Problem of Pain* in the *New York Herald Tribune*. Shuster, a layman who chaired the Notre Dame English department in the early 1920s, had then moved to New York City, where for several years he edited *Commonweal*. Two of his early essays in this journal had complained about the general weakness of American Catholic intellectual life.[11] When Shuster penned his Lewis review, he was serving as president of Hunter College of the City of New York. The review stated that Lewis's account of "a confluence of religious awe and the sense of moral obligation" succeeded in presenting "orthodox Christianity with unusual effectiveness." Moreover, the book "not only makes uncommon good sense, but it is great writing."[12]

In a later review in the same newspaper, another layman, Thomas Sugrue, praised *The Great Divorce* in similarly glowing terms: "Mr. Lewis is a scholar, a philosopher, and a most engaging writer, a combination so rare that it is hard to believe. But in one after another

---

[10]W. B. R. and P. M. S., reviews of *The Great Divorce* and *That Hideous Strength*, *Dominicana* 31 (June 1946): 149-51.

[11]On Shuster at Notre Dame and later, see Thomas E. Blantz, CSC, *The University of Notre Dame: A History* (Notre Dame, IN: University of Notre Dame Press, 2020), 261-63.

[12]George N. Shuster, review of *The Problem of Pain*, *New York Herald Tribune*, December 26, 1943, 6.

of his books . . . he has written with charm and humor about subjects supposed now to be beyond the reach of popular writing."[13] Five years after this review appeared, Sugrue's 1951 book, *A Catholic Speaks His Mind*, received a great deal of attention for arguing that Catholics should work more harmoniously with their Protestant neighbors.

Significantly, several priests responded just as positively to Lewis's work as these lay Catholics. In 1944, William Donaghy, SJ, then the associate editor of *America* and later president of Holy Cross College, called *Perelandra* "a superb communiqué on the ageless battle with powers and principalities." He also claimed to know "of no better portrayal of Evil than that achieved by Mr. Lewis." Donaghy conceded that "theologians may brood over some passages," but in his opinion the only conclusion could be that "this is . . . great literature."[14]

The attention that Father Harold Gardiner paid to Lewis was even more interesting.[15] Gardiner, also a Jesuit, studied English literature at Cambridge before becoming literary editor of *America* and then later a professor at the Catholic University of America, an editor of the *New Catholic Encyclopedia*, and chairman of the board for the Catholic Book Club. On the American publication of *That Hideous Strength*, Gardiner claimed about the entire Ransom Trilogy that "no multiple-decker among the literature of modern times" could compare with "Lewis' three in depth of spiritual insight and in dramatic interest." Gardiner did opine that *Perelandra* "remains to date Lewis' masterpiece," but for "spiritual insight that flashes out on page after page," *That Hideous Strength* "is a worthy successor, if not a peer."[16]

[13]Thomas Sugrue, review of *The Great Divorce*, *New York Herald Tribune Weekly Book Review*, March 1946, 4.

[14]William A. Donaghy, SJ, review of *Perelandra*, *America*, April 29, 1944, 104-5.

[15]For Gardiner's own account of his writing life, see Walter Romig, "Reverend Charles Harold Gardiner, S.J.," CatholicAuthors.com, www.catholicauthors.com/gardiner.html (accessed March 7, 2023).

[16]Harold Gardiner, SJ, review of *That Hideous Strength*, *America*, May 25, 1946, 157-58.

Earlier, Gardiner had praised Lewis's broadcast talks published as *Beyond Personality* just as enthusiastically but in a review with a telling sequel. In Gardiner's opinion, Lewis's account in that book of "matters like the Trinity and the whole magnificent sweep of our supernatural elevation in Christ" would "be a joy to Catholics (and whatever sincere Christians there are), a revelation to sincere seekers after religious truth, and a challenge to priests and other religious instructors." Gardiner did note that Lewis was silent "on the fact that our supernatural elevation comes through incorporation into Christ's church." Nonetheless, "these reservations apart, the book is shot through with a clear understanding of and a fine reverence for the truth and beauty of the supernatural."[17]

In response to this review, one of Gardiner's fellow Jesuits begged to differ. Philip Donnelly, SJ, quoted an English Catholic author to charge that Gardiner had failed to recognize a serious error in Lewis's book. According to Donnelly, Lewis based his account of "adoptive sonship" on believers' own "endeavors" rather than following proper Catholic doctrine, which depicted sonship as a supernatural state. Gardiner replied that he was glad to have this error identified but that he still felt Lewis had done a good job in treating "the supernatural in a wider sense, namely, the existence of God, the reality of sin, the Divinity of Christ, etc."[18]

In this brief exchange we catch a glimpse of the tension within the American church between expansive forces looking outward with Father Gardiner and defensive forces standing with Father Donnelly in support for tradition strictly defined. That tension, illustrated in contrasting responses to Lewis's work *between* different Catholics, also appeared *within* individual Catholics, with examples provided by a professor at Fordham and the only American Catholic woman to write on Lewis in this period.

---

[17] Harold Gardiner, SJ, review of *Beyond Personality*, *America*, May 25, 1945, 158-59.

[18] Philip J. Donnelly, SJ, and Harold Gardiner, SJ, "Protest on C. S. Lewis," *America*, June 30, 1945, 263. The critical article from England was G. D. Smith, "Nature and Spirit, According to a Recent Work," *The Clergy Review* (February 1945): 62-69.

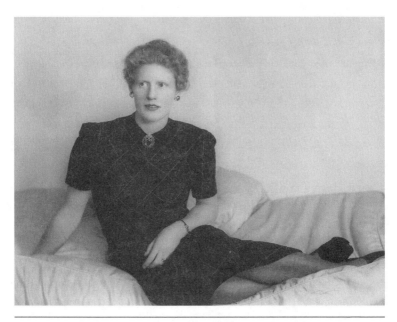

Figure 1.1. This 1938 portrait of Anne Jackson Fremantle was made in England before she moved to the United States and became one of C. S. Lewis's most discriminating Catholic readers.

That woman was Anne Jackson Fremantle, who was also the only English-born author and only one of two adult Catholic converts to review Lewis's books. Fremantle, a high-born supporter of leftist causes before her emigration to the United States in 1942, came into the church about the time of her arrival. She then went on to write for a number of Catholic and secular periodicals, to work for *Commonweal*, Fordham University, and the United Nations, and eventually to publish a number of books for Catholic readers.[19]

In the span of less than two years, Fremantle published three reviews, with especially kind words for how Lewis in *Beyond Personality*

---

[19]See Wolfgang Saxon, obituary for Anne Fremantle, *New York Times*, December 28, 2002. Her books included *Mothers: A Catholic Treasury of Great Stories* (1951), *Christian Conversation: Catholic Thought for Every Day of the Year* (1953), *The Age of Belief: The Medieval Philosophers* (1954), *The Papal Encyclicals* (1956), and, with a preface by W. H. Auden, *Protestant Mystics* (1964).

explained "predestination and foreknowledge" in ways with which "Saint Thomas Aquinas would have found no fault" and for how *That Hideous Strength* evoked Augustine's two cities (the City of Man and the City of God) with "terrifying and thriller-like actuality." She also obviously admired *The Abolition of Man* with what she called Lewis's attack on "the triumph of pragmatism" and his depiction of what, in defending objective moral values, Lewis called "This Way, the Tao of the Chinese, the Rta of Hinduism, the *ordo amoris* [way of love] of Augustine." Yet with approval came also critique. In Fremantle's opinion, *That Hideous Strength* was nowhere near as effective as Lewis's "theological perception" in *The Screwtape Letters* or *The Great Divorce*. More seriously, she faulted his depiction of Christian faith in *Beyond Personality* (which Harold Gardiner had praised so lavishly) as neglecting the "channels of grace" that sustain Christian life. In her words, Lewis offered "a picayune view of the Church. . . . She, who is the Whole Christ, who in her body, and in that of each one of her members, completes the Passion."[20]

John F. Dwyer, a professor at Fordham, responded more favorably in four reviews published in *Thought*, the monthly periodical sponsored by his Jesuit university, yet he also made a number of criticisms. Dwyer had nothing but praise for *The Screwtape Letters*, a "keen, shrewd and helpful" work that "appears flawless from the viewpoint of Catholic doctrine." Just as much, he liked *The Great Divorce*, which in high praise for a Catholic professor he called "Lewis' modest *Divina Comedia*" and his "new masterpiece." After commending the book's "literary excellence," Dwyer concluded that "it is a fantasy more subtle than *The Screwtape Letters* and rivaling that work in brilliance. There is the same keen psychological analysis of his

[20]Anne Fremantle, review of *Beyond Personality*, *Commonweal*, September 14, 1945, 528-29; Fremantle, review of *That Hideous Strength*, *New York Herald Tribune Weekly Book Review*, June 2, 1946, 12; Fremantle, review of *The Abolition of Man*, *Commonweal*, June 6, 1947, 193-94.

characters, but the biting satire is gone. Instead you feel the joy and happiness of the Bright Spirits, you share their keen pity for the foolish, self-willed ghosts who are their own damnation."[21]

When it came to Lewis's straightforward expositions of Christian faith, Dwyer continued to express appreciation but now alongside carefully phrased criticism. According to Dwyer, *The Case for Christianity* was admirable "as a layman's sincere and public confession of his faith" in which "nothing the author says contradicts Catholic teaching." But he also thought the book fell short because it merely recommended the words of Christ while allowing "the reader to take from Christ's words any meaning he wishes." This not-so-subtle response echoed Fremantle's complaint about Lewis's "picayune" attention to the church and the church's teaching. Concerning such teaching, Dwyer thought that *The Case for Christianity* made a serious error by not treating "fundamental" Christian doctrines such as the "full historicity of the Gospels" and "the inerrancy of the Bible as the word of God." Similarly, he opined about *The Problem of Pain* that although its "main thesis" was "beautiful and consoling," it was also "incomplete." According to Dwyer, Lewis did not say what needed to be said about "the nature and function of the human soul"; Lewis also implied that "the Bible . . . appears not to be inerrant." Dwyer ended this review, however, on a charitable note with the hope that "a vigorous thinker and ardent Christian like Mr. Lewis may be expected, if given time, to think these questions through to consistency" and so come to embrace "fully orthodox truth."[22]

It is noteworthy that the two longest, most learned, and most laudatory examples of Lewis criticism by any Americans in this period came from Catholics who seemed completely untroubled by the

---

[21]John F. Dwyer, review of *The Screwtape Letters, Thought* 18 (1943): 364; Dwyer, review of *The Great Divorce, Thought* 21 (1946): 746.

[22]John F. Dwyer, review of *The Case for Christianity, Thought* 19 (1944): 171; Dwyer, review of *The Problem of Pain, Thought* 19 (1944): 565.

Figure 1.2. A Canisius College professor of English, Charles Brady, was the first American writer to provide a full-orbed account of C. S. Lewis's literary work.

reservations other reviewers voiced. The first appeared in 1944 from a Canisius College professor whom Lewis congratulated as providing a comprehensive account of all his writings, the second in 1945 as a review-essay by a professor of English literature at Marquette who situated *Perelandra* in the context of much else that Lewis had written.

Charles Brady (1912–1995), a graduate of Canisius, a college founded by Jesuits, returned to teach at his alma mater after completing a master's degree at Harvard.[23] At age twenty-four, in 1936,

---

[23]Extensive obituaries were entered into the *Congressional Record* on May 11, 1995, by a New York congressman, John J. LaFalce, a Canisius alumnus who had studied with Brady;

he became chair of the English department, a position he held until 1959, after which Brady continued to teach for another twenty years and then remained an active book reviewer for the Buffalo *News* for still two more decades. As an author in his own right, Brady published poems, fiction for children (including *The Church Mouse of St. Nicholas* [1966], which told how an underweight church mouse inspired the beloved Christmas carol "Silent Night"), and historical novels based on the lives of Thomas More (1953) and Leif Erickson (1958). His anthology *A Catholic Reader*, published shortly after he wrote about Lewis, began with Brady explaining that, while "an embattled Church Militant" required polemical writing "since that far-off day when Martin Luther nailed his theses to the church door at Wittenberg," he wanted to show that Catholics could write sparkling fiction, exposition, poetry, anecdote, and essays that did not major in controversy.[24] His anthology included selections from priests such as John Henry Newman, Ronald Knox, and Harold Gardiner, SJ, but even more material from lay Catholics, including Thomas Malory, John Dryden, Alexander Pope, Hilaire Belloc, G. K. Chesterton, Evelyn Waugh, Clare Booth Luce, Thomas Merton, and Robert Lowell.

The Jesuits' magazine *America* published Brady's two essays, "Introduction to Lewis" and "C. S. Lewis: II," in 1944, the titles being the only humdrum thing about the articles.[25] In an immensely learned treatment, Brady explained how Lewis's academic writing on Percy Bysshe Shelley, Geoffrey Chaucer, and especially John Milton informed his works for popular audiences, such as *The Screwtape Letters*, which Brady called "the most phenomenally popular household book of applied religion of the twentieth century." He urged his readers, however, to go beyond this one work to other

see www.congress.gov/104/crec/1995/05/11/141/78/CREC-1995-05-11-pt1-PgE999.pdf (accessed April 3, 2023).

[24]Charles Brady, ed., *A Catholic Reader* (Buffalo, NY: Desmond & Stapleton, 1947), ix.

[25]For a transcription of these two articles, see the appendix.

writings, since Lewis was "the only truly popular champion of
Orthodoxy . . . in book, pamphlet and radio address since the passing
of Gilbert Keith Chesterton."[26] In praising the unobtrusive learning
behind such work, Brady claimed that the "pages" of Lewis's writing
constituted "a melodious sounding-board, a whispering-gallery . . . of
what is great in world literature." And then Brady specified as Lewis's
sources Virgil and the *Aeneid*, R. H. Benson, Olaf Stapledon, Rider
Haggard, Ronald Knox, J. R. R. Tolkien, William Morris, Jonathan
Swift, John Henry Newman, Chaucer, Dante Alighieri, and many
others including especially, again, Milton.[27]

In this tidal wave of commendation, no hint appeared that Brady
considered any aspect of Lewis's work questionable by Catholic standards. To the contrary, he contended that even "the non-professional
reader" would benefit from *The Personal Heresy* and the academic
essays gathered in Lewis's *Rehabilitations* because of their excellent
"humane scholarship." These works, according to Brady, revealed
Lewis as a "very humanistic, and therefore Catholic, don."[28] In other
words, since to a Roman Catholic "all truth is God's truth," and Lewis
wrote so truly about so many aspects of human experience, it was
appropriate to regard him as a Catholic.

Specifically Catholic concerns surfaced only once in these essays,
when Brady chided reviewers for treating *Out of the Silent Planet* and
Perelandra "very shabbily," including some "feckless" Catholic reviewers who missed the subtle defense of Christian orthodoxy in
these works.[29] For the rest, this first American to write comprehen-
sively about C. S. Lewis's books offered his glowing introduction in a
Catholic magazine with the express hope that more Catholic readers
would be drawn to those books.

---

[26]Charles A. Brady, "Introduction to Lewis," *America*, May 27, 1944, 213-14.
[27]Charles A. Brady, "C. S. Lewis: II," *America*, June 10, 1944, 270-71.
[28]Brady, "Introduction to Lewis," 214.
[29]Brady, "Introduction to Lewis," 214.

The review-essay on *Perelandra* by Marquette professor Victor M. Hamm (born 1904), which appeared just a year after Brady's comprehensive report, strained the limits of praise just as thoroughly. Hamm had earned degrees at Marquette and a PhD at Harvard before teaching briefly at two Catholic colleges and then returning to his alma mater, another school founded by Jesuits, where he taught for several decades. Known for his translations of fifteenth-century Italian philosopher Pico della Mirandola and for several works of literary criticism, Hamms's "Mr. Lewis in Perelandra" appeared in the Fordham quarterly *Thought*. It would be the longest American essay on a single work by Lewis for many years to come.

Hamm began arrestingly: "Milton wrote the epics of *Paradise Lost* and *Paradise Regained*. Mr. C. S. Lewis has essayed the epic of Paradise Retained." As did Brady, Hamm identified a host of obvious and not-so-obvious literary influences—H. G. Wells, Jules Verne, Rider Haggard, Plato, the Neoplatonists, the Kabbala, Rosicrucianism, Greek and Oriental myths, Shelley, John Keats, Robert Blake, Dante, and more—but all employed to craft an inspiring fiction and a bold Christian affirmation accessible to all readers. After outlining the plot, in which the protagonist, Ransom, acts to prevent Perelandra from falling into sin as Eve had fallen, Hamm summarized his assessment of Lewis's art and faith: "To some [Lewis's] sheer imaginative power will alone be enough to rank the novel among the great works of invention. . . . But beyond all this, the form that vivifies and organizes Mr. Lewis's art is his Christian faith which has given him the power to see as in a dream the incorporation of a futurable, the reality of a possibility."[30]

More than half of this essay then positioned *Perelandra* against Lewis's other imaginative works, especially his *Preface to Paradise Lost*, which, with Brady, Hamm considered the crucial academic framework

---

[30]Victor M. Hamm, "Mr. Lewis in Perelandra," *Thought* 20 (1945): 270-71, 276.

for the imaginative world of *Perelandra*. He brought his essay to a close by heralding Lewis's triumph with this moving evocation:

> The Universe is friendly, because it is filled with God and His angels. It is only our silent planet, which has cut itself off from communication with the great order by its act of primal disloyalty, that is an exile, and we the *exsules filii Hevae*, the exiled sons of Eve, weeping and wailing in this valley of tears, dreaming of happy sinless spheres in our unhappiness and making poems to ease the bitter sorrow of our hearts.[31]

Before turning to Catholic reviews that addressed primarily theological or philosophical questions, a pause is in order to take stock of the most obvious features of the main Catholic criticism. First, with near unanimity Catholics welcomed Lewis's works for their literary brio, academic depth, imaginative creativity, and forthright Christianity. Directly or indirectly, they expressed the opinion that his writings were fully compatible with Catholic teaching, except for how they neglected the importance of the church. Yet only some of the critics expressed that reservation. Many reviewers mentioned Lewis's lay status explicitly, or referenced it implicitly, by referring to him as "Mr." While praise mounted highest for *The Screwtape Letters*, *The Great Divorce*, and *Perelandra*, reviewers repeatedly criticized other works only because they did not come up to the excellence of these three. Lay Catholics outnumbered clerics as recommenders of Lewis's work, but not by much. The English professors Brady and Hamm made the most far-ranging assessments, particularly by showing that wide reading in ancient and modern authors made

---

[31]Hamm, "Mr. Lewis in Perelandra," 287. Lewis thanked Hamm when the professor sent him a copy of this essay but also gently corrected the reviewers' mistakes in reporting the languages (!) of the space novels; see C. S. Lewis to Victor M. Hamm, August 11, 1945, in Hooper, *Collected Letters* 2:666-67. Hamm's later review of *That Hideous Strength* was not as enthusiastic (he questioned the mix of realism and supernaturalism), yet it was still quite positive; see Victor M. Hamm, review of *That Hideous Strength*, *Thought* 21 (1946): 545-47.

Lewis's academic writing unusually convincing but that this same intellectual depth provided a sturdy foundation for the popular works' attractive breadth. To step back slightly for an observation about the context of these reviews, a variety of well-established Catholic periodicals provided ideal forums for wide-ranging discussion of Lewis's books.

It is important to remember that these early Catholic reviews appeared well before the Second Vatican Council. Catholicism was never as repressive, priest-ridden, monochrome, or oriented toward salvation by works as Protestants regularly complained. But the church was definitely traditional. It did regard all things Protestant or liberal in the political sense as posing serious threats. It remained in general much less open to the world beyond Catholic precincts than would be the case after the paradigm-shifting deliverances of the council that met from 1962 to 1965.

DOCTRINAL QUESTIONS

In that preconciliar world, American Catholic responses that featured matters of philosophical or theological principle were particularly revealing. What substantive matters did Catholics regard as potentially objectionable from this non-Catholic author? What drew their attention as gifts from Lewis for specifically Catholic ways of looking at the world?

Serious theological objection to Lewis came from only the most conservative corners of the American church. It appeared mostly in the *American Ecclesiastical Review*, a quarterly from the Catholic University of America, the educational institution in the American landscape most closely associated with Catholic traditionalism. A first expression of mild uneasiness appeared in a review of *Perelandra* from 1944. Father Joseph Clifford Fenton, professor of dogmatic theology at the Catholic University of America and editor of its *Review*, did not think *Perelandra* matched the excellence of *The Screwtape*

Letters, but he still praised it for recognizing the importance of "divine life." Fenton, however, did echo the complaint made earlier that "Mr. Lewis seems to lack only a definite affection of the true Church of Jesus Christ."[32]

Sharper criticism followed later that same year when the same periodical reviewed *The Problem of Pain*. Michael J. Gruenthaner, SJ, editor of *Catholic Biblical Quarterly*, acknowledged this book's "deep thought and . . . refreshing originality of treatment." Then, however, he went on to say that "the concept of the supernatural has eluded [Lewis] altogether" and that he erred by "interpret[ing] the fires of hell figuratively."[33]

More far-reaching objections soon appeared from another Jesuit, Malachi J. Donnelly, SJ, of St. Mary's College, Kansas. In a short review of *The Great Divorce* and a more extended assessment of *Beyond Personality*, Father Donnelly did not hesitate to acknowledge that Lewis's books "contain much good" and that Lewis was "a good man . . . who is sincere with regard to religious matters and in his personal and deep love for Jesus Christ." Yet Donnelly was troubled by the same mistake, as he saw it, that was noted in the objection to the positive review of *Beyond Personality* by Harold Gardiner, SJ. In a word, "Mr. Lewis' doctrine of divine adoption . . . is not in full accord with Catholic doctrine."[34]

If Donnelly was somewhat troubled by Lewis, however, he was bothered even more by Catholics who ignored a provision in the church's canon law (canon 1399) that required reviewers of theological books by non-Catholic authors to warn Catholic readers away

---

[32]Joseph Clifford Fenton, review of *Perelandra*, *American Ecclesiastical Review* 110 (June 1944): 477.

[33]Michael J. Gruenthaner, SJ, review of *The Problem of Pain*, *American Ecclesiastical Review* 111 (October 1944): 312-13.

[34]Malachi J. Donnelly, SJ, review of *The Great Divorce*, *Theological Studies* 7 (1946): 495; Donnelly, "Church Law and Non-Catholic Books," *American Ecclesiastical Review* 114 (June 1946): 406-7.

from these books "unless the reviewer is morally certain that there is nothing in the book contrary to our Catholic faith." On that score, Lewis's *Beyond Personality* clearly did not measure up: the book "teaches and is largely founded on a false doctrine of the supernatural life; it is tainted with modernistic tendencies with regard to divine Revelation and the Church; and . . . it has a distinct inclination (in some respects) towards religious indifferentism."[35] Despite those errors, Donnelly was aghast that "among four of the more prominent Catholic periodicals . . . , we have found that *Beyond Personality* was enthusiastically reviewed, to such an extent that the ordinary Catholic would have gotten the idea that there was nothing within the covers of this book that might be contrary to his Catholic faith." Especially for works from authors such as Lewis with some admittedly positive qualities, Donnelly insisted that Catholic reviewers simply had to exercise "cautious prudence" when reviewing "the book of a non-Catholic who writes . . . on religion."[36]

These objections to Lewis's theology and the worry about Catholics reviewing his books without discrimination represented, however, a decidedly minority opinion, even when it came to specific doctrinal questions. Much more strongly and much more often, American Catholic writers stressed how often Lewis's defense of objective truth and especially his depiction of humankind's innate moral consciousness reinforced fundamental Catholic teaching.

One of the earliest and most intriguing Catholic responses to Lewis came when Thomas Merton published a substantial review of *The Personal Heresy* in the *New York Times*. It was published in July 1939, less than a year after Merton had sought Catholic baptism and

---

[35]For Catholics, "religious indifferentism" designated all teaching that did not view Catholicism as the one true religion.

[36]Donnelly, "Church Law," 403, 406-9. The complaint about Catholic reviewers also appeared in Donnelly, review of *The Great Divorce*, 495. Three of the positive reviews to which Donnelly referred were almost certainly those found in *America, Catholic World,* and *Commonweal.* I have not located the fourth.

Figure 1.3. Thomas Merton reviewed the Lewis-Tillyard debate over how critics should assess the relationship of authors to their works before either he or Lewis achieved the renown they would both soon enjoy.

eighteen months before he began his celebrated monastic career at the Trappist Abbey of Our Lady of Gethsemani in Kentucky. In that jointly authored book, Lewis tried to convince his literary antagonist, E. M. W. Tillyard, that a poem should be read for what it said about the object of the poem rather than about the poet. In his review, Merton contended that Lewis used "the term 'heresy' not ironically but in the technical Catholic sense" when arguing against the "personal heresy."[37] Whether or not Lewis intended to be that specific, the Catholic convert recognized a theological message in Lewis's literary work that few readers then, and not too many since, have been able

---

[37]Thomas Merton, review of *The Personal Heresy*, *New York Times*, July 9, 1939, 16-17, here 16.

to spell out so clearly. It is the message that human insights, achievements, and breakthroughs are best understood as reflecting an external reality rather than the genius of the human author. In his biography of Merton, Lawrence Cunningham specified the connection between this commendation of Lewis's defense of literary objectivity and Merton's later fascination with Chinese Taoist philosophy. Merton, according to Cunningham, "simply read the ancient Taoist masters . . . in the same spirit that Saint Augustine read Plotinus or Saint Thomas Aquinas read Aristotle."[38] In this assessment, Merton's later fascination with Chinese thought that postulated universal and objective moral principles only repeated how key figures in the history of orthodox Catholic theology depicted Christianity as clarifying, focusing, and fulfilling by revelation what the best non-Christian thinkers had found in nature.

A recent book on Lewis's articulation of natural-law doctrine details how "a defense of objective moral principles, universal in application, and knowable by reason, would become a central thread in nearly all of Lewis' writings."[39] Precisely that defense excited early American Catholic reviewers, who read in Lewis's accounts of reason, the moral life, and Christian faith an effective modern articulation of fundamental Catholic theology.

On September 7, 1943, Macmillan in New York published *The Case for Christianity*. In this edition of Lewis's first broadcast talks he spoke much about natural law, or what he called "the Law of Human Nature." In the issue of *America* dated only eleven days later (September 18), a reviewer praised the book for how "Mr. Lewis, with irresistible logic, leads us to the universal Natural Law, our fallen condition and the existence of the supernatural," and then "shows

[38]Lawrence S. Cunningham, *Thomas Merton: The Monastic Vision* (Grand Rapids: Eerdmans, 1999), 118.
[39]Micah J. Watson and Justin B. Dyer, *C. S. Lewis on Politics and Natural Law* (New York: Cambridge University Press, 2016), 44.

Christianity as the most satisfying answer to our human dilemmas." Before the end of the year, Father James J. Maguire, CSP, hailed the book in the Paulists' *Catholic World* for "the timeliness of this gem of apologetics" with "its emphasis on the fundamental needs of man regarded as a moral being." In recounting that for Lewis personally, the "re-discovery of the moral law was his gateway to Christ," Maguire conceded that this publication was "not the book that, in every detail, a Catholic would have written." He nonetheless ended by concluding that it said "very many things that desperately need to be said." As "armies of men are groping their way back to the religion of Christ, this book will facilitate greatly that sacred journey."[40] In 1947, when *The Abolition of Man* appeared, Lewis expanded his exposition of natural law, which in that work he called the Tao. Even Anne Fremantle, who had hesitated to endorse Lewis wholeheartedly, commended his emphasis in that work on "objective reality."[41]

For American Catholics, Lewis's defense of natural law, or what he called the Tao in his *Abolition of Man*, exerted a sustained influence. Ten years after *The Abolition of Man* was published, Notre Dame professor Leo Ward cited that book as a key text in a paper delivered to the American Philosophical Association. As one of the most respected Catholic philosophers of the day, Ward was documenting what he called "The 'Natural Law' Rebound." In Ward's view, "the broad contemporary fact of totalitarianism" had led to the rejection of John Dewey's morally relativistic pragmatism and a "present-day affirmation of ethical universalism." Ward cited many contemporaries—some Catholic, such as Jacques Maritain, and others secular—who were defending universal moral objectivity. He then wrote, "For our part we take the statement of natural law by C. S. Lewis in *The Abolition of Man*

---

[40]Charles Keenan, review of *The Case for Christianity, America*, September 18, 1943, 664; James J. Maguire, review of *The Case for Christianity, Catholic World* 143 (November 1943): 215-16.
[41]Anne Fremantle, review of *The Abolition of Man, Commonweal*, June 6, 1947, 194; see above for her fuller comment on this book.

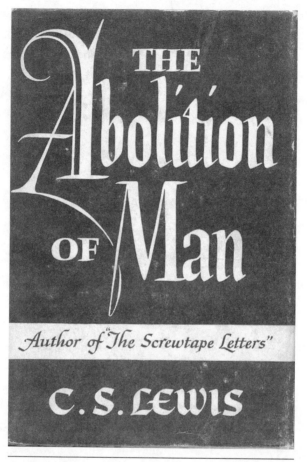

Figure 1.4. In this book, Lewis offered an account of the "Tao," or the universal human recognition of objective moral value, that resonated with teachings in Catholic doctrine and philosophy about natural law.

as the most thoroughly existential and contextual statement in recent times." To Ward, Lewis had restated persuasively a foundational principle of Catholic moral philosophy better than recent Catholic authors, who "were . . . thought, and sometimes rightly thought, to be dogmatic" rather than philosophically attuned.[42]

---

[42]Leo R. Ward, "The 'Natural Law' Rebound," *Review of Politics* 21 (January 1959): 114, 116, 118.

An intriguing sidelight accompanied positive Catholic response to *The Abolition of Man.* The author of a short but glowing review in the Jesuits' weekly, *America,* was Father John LaFarge, himself a Jesuit. LaFarge heartily endorsed Lewis's prediction of impending disaster should humankind ever give up the belief in objective moral values. He concluded that Lewis "writes with his customary vigor, shrewdness, simplicity. I recommend the little volume for any thoughtful man's pocket and any motherly woman's handbag."[43] Before writing this review, LaFarge, as shown in books by Karen Johnson and John McGreevy, led Catholic clerics in campaigning for racial justice in society and the integration of African Americans into the full life of the church.[44]

Two details connect LaFarge's review to the racial challenge confronting American Catholicism. That challenge came from the fact that some priests, such as LaFarge, and even more nuns had taken the lead in promoting civil rights. But many urban White Catholics and often their parish priests resisted—sometimes violently—efforts to integrate the churches and schools their immigrant communities had built for themselves with great sacrifice. The first detail, supplied by Karen Johnson, concerns LaFarge's attitude toward the laity. Although he was a leading progressive on race, LaFarge remained traditional in assuming that guidance for the church's social outreach should remain firmly in the control of bishops and priests. The laity could help but never lead.

The other detail takes us back to Charles Brady's comprehensive review of Lewis's work. As an aside, Brady praised one particular scene from *Out of the Silent Planet.* It was "the strangely moving encounter between Ransom and the *hrossa*—which can be

[43]John LaFarge, review of *The Abolition of Man, America,* April 12, 1947, 51.
[44]Johnson, *One in Christ,* 4, 30, 113, 129; John T. McGreevy, *Parish Boundaries: The Catholic Encounter with Race in the Twentieth-Century Urban North* (Chicago: University of Chicago Press, 1996), 41, 106.

interpreted . . . as an allegory of racial fear and repugnance and its sublimation into deep affection through the very recognition of the fact of difference."[45] As it happened, Brady's interpretation of this passage surprised Lewis himself, who in thanking Brady for his essays wrote, "When you talk about meetings of human races in connexion with Ransom and the Hrossa you say something that was not in my mind at all. So much the better: a book's not worth writing unless it suggests more than the author intended."[46] A possibility that did not register for Lewis an American Catholic reviewer picked up as relevant for his church's challenge of reconciliation between not different races on Mars but different races in Chicago, Detroit, and Milwaukee.

CONCLUSION

It should be clear why Lewis's early American reception proved especially significant for the nation's Catholics. As a first instance, their church was tied to a vision of authority that viewed it emanating almost exclusively from on high. Yet in modern America, lay Catholics were increasingly well educated, they had exercised an expanding range of free choices, and in many cases they were eager to help shape the church's internal spiritual life and expand its outreach into society. Much else transpired before one of the Second Vatican Council's most important documents, its Dogmatic Constitution on the Church (*Lumen Gentium*), stressed the central importance of the laity in constituting "the people of God." But the enthusiastic commendation of a British layman for his compelling contributions to Christian witness marked a clear step toward fuller Catholic empowerment of the laity.

Because this layman was not himself a Catholic, the warm response he received also pointed to the day when the once nearly

---

[45]Brady, "C. S. Lewis: II," 269.
[46]C. S. Lewis to Brady, in Hooper, *Collected Letters* 2:630.

impregnable barriers between Catholics and other Christians would crumble, not falling all the way down but becoming much less imposing and much more permeable. If a substantial number of reviewers qualified their commendations by noting that Lewis was not "one of theirs," all but a very few who offered that reservation treated it as a secondary concern. Others, such as the professors Brady and Hamm, seemed already to be fully supporting the deliberate downplaying of ecclesiastical differences that Lewis would later call "mere Christianity."

The number of Jesuits who wrote favorably about Lewis or who opened their periodicals for favorable commentary also deserves comment. In their American history, Catholics did not simply replicate European educational patterns, in large part because of the great effort required to serve the immigrant poor and then carve out a secure foothold in a dominantly Protestant culture. But by 1893 the Jesuits were sponsoring twenty-five colleges; many other religious orders and many local dioceses had contributed to the impressive number of 357 Catholic colleges founded during the second half of the nineteenth century. In Jesuit institutions and some of the others, the ideals of a thorough classical education eventually took hold. Their model, as summarized by John McGreevy, was the Jesuits' *Ratio Studiorum*, which prepared students for fluency in Latin, led advanced scholars into Greek, and prescribed regular study of Cicero, Homer, Virgil, Horace, and other classical authors.[47] The same program of studies featured a version of Thomas Aquinas on natural law understood as preparation for the full Christian revelation. As the twentieth century progressed, the curriculum at advanced centers of Catholic higher education broadened but did so while preserving a

---

[47] See John T. McGreevy, *American Jesuits and the World: How an Embattled Religious Order Made Modern Catholicism Global* (Princeton, NJ: Princeton University Press, 2016), 149-51, 153-54. For a comprehensive picture of the intellectual history of Catholic higher education in this era, see Gleason, *Contending with Modernity*.

great deal of what had gone before. Even into midcentury, however, this education was focused inwardly on preparing boys for possible vocations as priests or outwardly on preparing Catholic gentlemen who could give the lie to Protestant assumptions about the corrupting character of Catholic faith.

This educational background puts in perspective the enthusiasm that greeted Lewis from *America* magazine and Fordham's monthly journal *Thought*, that witnessed highly complimentary reviews from the Jesuit Fathers Gardiner, Donaghy, and LaForge, and that led to the trailblazing essays from Charles Brady at the Jesuits' Canisius and Victor Hamm at the Jesuits' Marquette. To be sure, a few Jesuits did uphold older standards in warning the faithful away from Lewis. But in the larger picture, commendation overwhelmed reservation. All who valued their education from Jesuits or at institutions aspiring to similarly high standards valued their first-rate classical training, and most also accepted the church's commitment to natural-law philosophy and theology. We do not have to imagine the delight such ones might experience when they read books by someone with learning just as deep as their own and a fresh defense of objective universal morality—but that also ranged more widely and was put to use with unusual creativity for both the Enlightenment of the learned and the Christian encouragement of the hoi polloi. We do not have to imagine, because that is how they responded to C. S. Lewis.

There is, finally, the bridge between Lewis and Catholics constructed by how he emphasized the natural law. As we will see in chapter three, that emphasis caused some Reformed evangelicals to withhold their full approval of Lewis's works. But for Catholics, it was an unexpected blessing from an unexpected quarter.

It would be incorrect to view the early Catholic reception of C. S. Lewis as dramatically influential in shaping the course of the American church. By no means have I canvassed all relevant Catholic scholarship for the World War II era. But from fairly wide reading,

I have found only one passing reference to Lewis (to how a Jesuit scholar in 1943 "enjoyed identifying non-Catholics as Mortimer Adler and C. S. Lewis as fellow-traveling defenders of 'an absolute moral order'").[48]

Instead, Catholic writing about Lewis can be viewed as testifying to subterranean changes underway. In the late 1940s the church seemed timeless, fixed, and immutable. Yet tremors underground were pointing to a new day for lay Catholic initiatives, a new season of edifying engagement with the world beyond the church's walls, and a time when some who were not Catholic joined in defending universal moral reason. For registering these tremors, the Catholic reception of C. S. Lewis served as a remarkably prescient seismograph.

---

[48]John C. Ford, SJ, "Notes on Moral Theology," *Theological Studies* 4 (December 1943): 562-63, as cited in McGreevy, *Catholicism and American Freedom*, 222. Besides the works of American Catholic history already cited, other outstanding books with no mention of Lewis include James Hennesey, SJ, *American Catholics: A History of the Roman Catholic Community in the United States* (New York: Oxford University Press, 1981); Jay P. Dolan, *The American Catholic Experience: A History from Colonial Times to the Present* (New York: Doubleday, 1985); Philip Gleason, *Keeping the Faith: American Catholicism Past and Present* (Notre Dame, IN: University of Notre Dame Press, 1987); Gerald P. Fogarty, SJ, *American Catholic Biblical Scholarship: A History from the Early Republic to Vatican II* (San Francisco: Harper & Row, 1989); John T. Noonan Jr., *A Church That Can and Cannot Change* (Notre Dame, IN: University of Notre Dame Press, 2005); and Leslie Woodcock Tentler, *American Catholics: A History* (New Haven, CT: Yale University Press, 2020).

RESPONSE

KAREN J. JOHNSON

RACE HAS SHAPED RELIGION IN AMERICA. From settlers' interactions with Native Americans, to justification for and resistance to chattel slavery, to the complicated development and maintenance of segregated churches, race has mattered.[1] Race also influenced Catholic readers of C. S. Lewis's work in the 1930s and 1940s. But how? And to what extent does race matter for understanding what Catholic responses to C. S. Lewis's writing reveal about the nature of Catholicism in America? The significance of race to Mark Noll's particular set of questions seems limited at first glance. After all, only one Catholic responding to Lewis, Charles Brady, tied Lewis's work to race. Digging a little deeper reveals that only two others, Father John LaFarge and Thomas Merton, led in any substantial way on racial issues. But just because Catholic reviewers did not talk about race does not mean that race was insignificant. Part of race's power is that it hides in plain sight. Contextualizing the Catholic authors who evaluated Lewis's work in the changing racial dynamics of their place, time, and faith not only teases out how race was functioning, it also accounts for more complexity in the "subterranean changes" at work in what Noll calls above the seemingly "timeless, fixed, and immutable" Catholic Church as laypeople increasingly exercised their voices.

Considering the places from which reviewers wrote reveals their racialized contexts. Many of Lewis's reviewers lived in northern cities, alongside most Catholics in the United States. In the 1910s, Black

---

[1] For Mark Noll's work on race and Christianity, see Mark A. Noll, *God and Race in American Politics* (Princeton, NJ: Princeton University Press, 2009).

migrants from the South made these cities their destination. The hope of a northern promised land where they could earn decent wages in industrial jobs and be seen by others as fully human led these men and women to leave Jim Crow tyranny.[2] The migrants moved to Washington, DC, home of Catholic University of America professor Father Joseph Clifford Fenton and layperson Anne Fremantle.[3] They moved to New York City, home of Father Bernard Conway, George Shuster, interracialist priest John LaFarge, and Fordham professor John Dwyer. They moved to Rochester, New York, where Canisius College professor Charles Brady worked, and to Milwaukee, home of Marquette professor Victor Hamm. They also moved to Chicago; Gary, Indiana; and Kansas City, centers of migration near to reviewers living outside major urban centers, such as Father Malachi J. Donnelly of St. Mary's College in Kansas and William Donaghy of the University of Notre Dame.

In these cities and others, the Great Migration initiated a crisis for White Catholics. Although few of Lewis's reviewers spent their days engaged in racial matters, they could not avoid the changing racial dynamics in their cities. They were members of a church that preached the unity of all people in Christ, no matter their race. And they were members of a church that actively discriminated against African Americans—Catholic and non-Catholic alike. During this era, laypeople led a minority of Black and White Catholics in an interracial justice mission. When they said they were working for interracial justice, they meant bringing their faith to bear on broken economic and social systems preventing African Americans' full flourishing. They targeted the housing market, jobs, education, and

---

[2]For the Great Migration, see James R. Grossman, *Land of Hope: Chicago, Black Southerners and the Great Migration* (Chicago: University of Chicago Press, 1991); Isabel Wilkerson, *The Warmth of Other Suns: The Epic Story of America's Great Migration* (New York: Random House, 2010).

[3]Fremantle lived in Washington, DC, when she wrote some of her reviews of Lewis's books, until she moved to New York City in 1947.

parish life.[4] They insisted, too, that they must execute this work together, with African American and White people working side by side.

Since many Black migrants from the evangelical Bible Belt found Catholicism appealing, Black Catholic faith in the North was a story of conversion.[5] Several migrants became Catholic because the Catholic schools offered a better education compared to the overcrowded public schools that most African American children attended. Black families did not have to be Catholic to send their children to Catholic school, but parishes required that they take catechesis classes, which led many to the faith. The recent converts enjoyed the quiet, dignified worship.[6] They also appreciated that Catholic theology was racially inclusive, at least in theory. In the South, White Protestants' faith supported segregation. For their White Christian neighbors from down South, racial segregation was God's will. White southern Christians believed that if a Black person did not stay in their place, they should expect negative repercussions.[7] And if a White man beat an "uppity" Black man on Saturday night, that White man need not repent on Sunday morning in church.

Catholic social thought, however, demanded justice on earth. It had emerged in the decades prior to the Great Migration, during the turbulence of the Industrial Revolution, as Catholics grappled with

[4]See Karen J. Johnson, *One in Christ: Chicago Catholics and the Quest for Interracial Justice* (New York: Oxford University Press, 2018); John T. McGreevy, *Parish Boundaries: The Catholic Encounter with Race in the Twentieth-Century Urban North* (Chicago: University of Chicago Press, 1996); Timothy Neary, *Crossing Parish Boundaries: Race, Sports, and Catholic Youth in Chicago, 1914–1954* (Chicago: University of Chicago Press, 2016).
[5]Neary, *Crossing Parish Boundaries*; Matthew J. Cressler, *Authentically Black and Truly Catholic: The Rise of Black Catholicism in the Great Migration* (New York: New York University Press, 2017).
[6]Cressler, *Authentically Black and Truly Catholic*, chap. 2.
[7]J. Russell Hawkins, *Because the Bible Told Them So: How Southern Evangelicals Fought to Preserve White Supremacy* (New York: Oxford University Press, 2021); Carolyn Renée Dupont, *Mississippi Praying: Southern White Evangelicals and the Civil Rights Movement, 1945–1975* (New York: New York University Press, 2013); Paul Harvey, *Bounds of Their Habitation: Race and Religion in American History* (New York: Rowman & Littlefield, 2016); Ansley Lillian Quiros, *God with Us: Lived Theology and the Freedom Struggle in Americus, Georgia, 1942–1976* (Chapel Hill: University of North Carolina Press, 2018).

the poverty wrought by urbanization and industrialization. Catholic leaders sought a third way between unfettered capitalism and communism that would lead to the flourishing of workers and owners alike. Catholic social thought emphasized each group's responsibility to care for one another because they were united in Christ.[8] Catholic interracialists applied the principles of Catholic social thought to their own complicated racial context. But among Catholics in the North, they were the minority.

Black Catholics born in the North and raised in the church knew the real truth about the Catholic Church: that it was not living up to its own theological promises of unity and justice. Their converted brethren soon discovered this fact. Because of the White Catholic hierarchy's racial exclusion, few priests were African American, and the church (although often unintentionally) was helping to create a racial dyad in the cities, with White people on top and African Americans on the bottom. As Black migrants moved North, they came to cities peopled by members of the different White races. Early twentieth-century folks understood Italians, Lithuanians, Poles, and others as separate races. Negroes, to use the language of the time, were one of many races, even if members of White racial groups assumed their own superiority. However, the growing presence of African Americans in northern cities coupled with the precipitous drop in foreign immigration by the 1920s melted the different White races into *one* White race, as opposed to the so-called Negro race.[9]

Catholicism contributed to the North not living up to Black migrants' expectations. In some ways, of course, the North was better

---

[8]The most cited statement on Catholic social thought is Leo XIII, *Rerum Novarum*, 1891, www.vatican.va/holy_father/leo_xiii/encyclicals/documents/hf_l-xiii_enc_15051891_rerum-novarum_en.html.

[9]For debates over how Whiteness functioned, see Matthew Frye Jacobson, *Whiteness of a Different Color* (Cambridge, MA: Harvard University Press, 1998); David R. Roediger, *The Wages of Whiteness: Race and the Making of the American Working Class* (London: Verso, 2007); Johnson, *One in Christ*, chap. 1.

than the South—African Americans could vote, for instance, and sit wherever they wanted on the bus. But often, their dreams of a promised land shriveled like a raisin in the sun. When new Black residents moved into communities, they found *some* White people willing to embrace them. As Noll observes, however, many White Catholics opposed their Black neighbors. White people used restrictive covenants or outright violence to resist Black neighbors' presence.[10] While individual prejudice contributed to White Catholics' resistance, larger religious and economic systems also lessened the appeal of Black neighbors.

The larger racial-economic dynamics influencing White Catholics included government-sanctioned redlining, which resisted integrated housing. Redlining began during the Great Depression, during the years the Catholic printing house Sheed & Ward published the first edition of Lewis's *The Pilgrim's Regress.* Incidentally, Frank Sheed and Maisie Ward were friends with several Catholic interracialists. But neither they nor their interracialist friends knew the racial implications of how the US government worked to stop foreclosures. Two governmental organizations, the Home Owners Loan Corporation and the Federal Housing Authority, created a series of maps that used discriminatory logic to label minority-owned and interracial neighborhoods as dangerous places to make loans. Although, by the 1940s, some scholars proved that White homeowners defaulted on their mortgages more often than Black homeowners, these deep, racialized economic assumptions became inscribed in the landscape, and their power became a self-reinforcing mechanism. Banks used these maps to make mortgage decisions and excluded African Americans from the booming postwar housing market. Simultaneously, housing

---

[10]Arnold Hirsch, "Massive Resistance in the Urban North: Trumbull Park, Chicago, 1953–1966," *The Journal of American History* 82, no. 2 (September 1995): 522-50; Arnold R. Hirsch, *Making the Second Ghetto: Race and Housing in Chicago, 1940–1960* (Chicago: University of Chicago Press, 1998).

became a key wealth-building tool for White homeowners. By the 1950s, this dynamic led to a secondary, exploitative mortgage market based on contract buying that was lucrative for White investors.[11]

Within this racialized economic context, many parish priests led efforts to resist integration to "protect" their parishes. Personal racial prejudice and the concern that Black neighbors would harm parish life shaped the priests' behavior. While the personal prejudice mattered, the racialized concerns for parish life reveal the complicated nature of race in northern cities. Priests had a strong theology of place and encouraged their working-class parishioners to buy their homes. For many White priests and laypeople, a Black neighbor signaled the demise of the parish for religious and economic reasons. Black neighbors were often Protestants, and while some converted to Catholicism, the majority maintained their Protestant faith. Black neighbors, therefore, would not contribute to the parish. White Catholics also saw Black neighbors as harbingers of falling home prices and therefore felt the need to sell their houses quickly, to move to a more economically stable neighborhood. Block-busting realtors used fear tactics to convince White homeowners to hurriedly sell at a low price. These realtors then made a profit when they sold the houses to Black buyers. If a young White couple actually wanted to buy a home in a changing neighborhood, mortgage money would soon dry up because of redlining.[12] No matter their personal prejudice, however, White Catholics contributed to the creation of Black ghettoes: narrow strips of land where African Americans paid higher prices than White people for inferior housing.[13]

---

[11]Kenneth T. Jackson, *Crabgrass Frontier: The Suburbanization of the United States* (New York: Oxford University Press, 1987); Beryl Satter, *Family Properties: Race, Real Estate, and the Exploitation of Black Urban America* (New York: Metropolitan Books, 2009).

[12]McGreevy, *Parish Boundaries*.

[13]For the bishops' reticence to support interracial justice, see Johnson, *One in Christ*; Bryan N. Massingale, *Racial Justice and the Catholic Church* (Maryknoll, NY: Orbis Books, 2010). While the issue was similarly complicated, few White Protestants supported housing integration. See, for instance, Mark T. Mulder, *Shades of White Flight: Evangelical*

LAY ACTION

These racial and economic dynamics shaped the cities Lewis's reviewers inhabited. But there was another factor at play: the way laypeople and priests related to one another. Lay-clergy interactions
complicated the racialized economic dynamics at the neighborhood
level, and those dynamics were changing during the 1930s and 1940s.
Noll argues that changes in how Catholics perceived the laity's role in
the world also contributed to *how* Catholic reviewers—both lay and
priest—engaged with the Protestant Lewis. Catholic engagement
with racial changes in their cities sheds further light on the increasing
lay initiative represented in the lay Catholic responses to Lewis.

Despite the limited support for interracial justice among Catholic
leaders, laypeople such as Black Catholic medical doctor Arthur G.
Falls toiled to recruit young Catholics to work for interracial justice.[14]
Many of his recruits were White, and they were part of a generation
that believed they could change the world for Christ. They cared
about the rights of labor, racial discrimination, urban decline, and
the rise of communism, and they were confident that laypeople and
priests together could help make the world better.[15] Some became
priests, but most worked to share the love of God with their neighbors
simply as parents, labor organizers, public servants, businesspeople,
writers, activists, and homeowners. Their confidence in their ability
as Catholics to bring the love of Christ to bear on significant social
issues was a far cry from their parents' views of the laity. Earlier

Congregations and Urban Departure (New Brunswick, NJ: Rutgers University Press,
2015); Mark Mulder, "Evangelical Church Polity and the Nuances of White Flight," *Journal
of Urban History* 38, no. 16 (2012): 16-38; Darren Dochuk, "'Praying for a Wicked City':
Congregation, Community and the Suburbanization of Fundamentalism," *Religion and
American Culture* 13, no. 2 (2003): 167-203.

[14]For more on Falls, see Lincoln Rice, "Confronting the Heresy of the 'Mythical Body of
Christ': The Life of Dr. Arthur Falls," *American Catholic Studies* 123, no. 2 (Summer 2012):
59-77; Rice, *Healing the Racial Divide: A Catholic Racial Justice Framework Inspired by Dr.
Arthur G. Falls* (Eugene, OR: Pickwick, 2014); Johnson, *One in Christ.*

[15]Steven M. Avella, *This Confident Church: Catholic Leadership and Life in Chicago, 1940–
1965* (Notre Dame, IN: University of Notre Dame Press, 1992).

generations saw their role as "paying, praying, and obeying" their priests, and many priests, bishops, and laypeople into the 1950s and 1960s continued to see that as constituting a layperson's life of faith.

This new breed of laypeople and their priestly allies justified their actions using the doctrine of the mystical body of Christ. Based in New Testament Scripture that depicts members of the church as members of Christ's body, the doctrine means Catholics are Jesus' actual hands and feet in the world. They are also ontologically united with other members, a unity in Christ that matters profoundly. Last, because God is outside time and Catholics do not know whether or when a person might become a member of Christ's body, when they serve another person, they could actually be serving Christ.

Two other streams of Catholicism further illustrate laypeople's changing conceptions of what it meant to be a faithful Catholic. Catholic Action, which emerged in Europe during the nineteenth-century labor conflicts, emphasized lay participation in the church's mission. Those priests who saw the laity as more than just a "paying, praying, and obeying" people taught high school students, college students, and young workers to see a situation, judge what was right or wrong in it, and act based on what they thought an appropriate Christian response should be. The key here is that Catholics were integrating their faith with their learning and work. In the fields of race relations, for instance, Catholic doctor Arthur Falls saw the higher tuberculosis death rates among African Americans. He judged that the deaths were not due to an inherent racial inferiority but rather to slum conditions caused by inconsistent garbage pickup, few housing options outside the ghetto for Black citizens, and little enforcement of building codes. Then he acted, partnering with the director of the Municipal Tuberculosis Sanatorium to advocate for systemic changes.[16] Falls was seeing, judging, and acting as part of his Catholic faith.

---

[16]Tuberculosis was a major issue in Chicago in the 1920s. There are several newspaper articles discussing the higher death rates among African Americans in the *Chicago*

The Catholic Worker Movement offers an additional example of changing conceptions of how laypeople's faith should influence their lives. The movement was founded in 1933 by Peter Maurin and Dorothy Day in New York City, and members wanted to "make the kind of society where it is easier to be good."[17] They saw Christ in other people, opening their doors to the indigent, feeding the hungry, and writing about African American concerns as on par with those of White workers (a fact Arthur Falls celebrated and then emphasized when he founded a Catholic Worker house in Chicago). They believed that if a man or woman had a place to sleep, was well fed, and seen with dignity, that person would do good things for others and find it easier to know God. As Day observed, "One needs to be happy in order to be good, and one needs to be good in order to be happy. One needs Christians in order to make a Christian social order, and one needs a Christian social order in order to raise Christians." This circle was a paradox, but "Christians are so full of the paradoxes. Such as dying to live. No one pretends that it is a simple matter. It is all very hard to understand."[18] Yet Catholics such as those associated with the Catholic worker stepped into the paradox and sought to leaven society with the love of God.

These examples illustrate the growing expertise of lay Catholics acting *as Catholics* in their respective fields, whether working for interracial justice, addressing poverty, or reviewing C. S. Lewis's work. In this framework, members of the Catholic hierarchy supported but did not usurp laypeople in their areas of expertise. Conflict, of course, infused this transition, as priests who had been trained and socialized to see their religious authority as final found that some laypeople would not obey. The conflict was complicated, as priests and laypeople were sometimes working toward the same end.

Defender, the city's leading African American newspaper. For Falls's involvement, see Arthur Falls, "Memoir Manuscript," 1962, in Marquette University Archives, 276-77.
[17]Dorothy Day, "On Pilgrimage," *The Catholic Worker* (February 1951), 1, 6.
[18]Day, "On Pilgrimage."

For example, interracialist priest John LaFarge hesitated to trust lay leadership, especially in his early career. In the early 1930s, LaFarge helped to engineer a priestly takeover of Federated Colored Catholics, a national, Black, lay-led group. Complicated debates surrounded this takeover: Should the organization prioritize interracialism or Black advancement? Were those two mutually exclusive? Should laypeople or priests be in charge? Some Black laypeople sided with LaFarge and his fellow priest, William Markoe, who was a White man. Others sided with the federation's lay leader, Thomas Wyatt Turner, an African American. Historians debate the extent to which LaFarge's and Markoe's concerns were racial (they thought African American leadership was problematic) or hierarchical (they did not trust lay leadership). Many Black lay Catholics supported LaFarge and Markoe for various reasons, one of which was that they thought they needed priests to improve African Americans' situation in the Catholic Church and improve African Americans' lives in the broader society.[19]

But even as these Black lay Catholics supported the White priests in the Federated Colored Catholics conflict, they also followed the mystical body's doctrine by promoting interracial justice in their churches, workplaces, and schools, even though their actions often countered other priests' explicit desires. At the national level, however, the Federated Colored Catholic organization languished after LaFarge's and Markoe's priestly takeover. Almost thirty years later, the laypeople applied what they learned from the Federated Colored Catholics conflict when Chicago's lay-led Catholic Interracial Council founded the National Catholic Conference for Interracial Justice, the first national organization since the Federated Colored Catholics to unite Catholics working on racial issues. The laypeople and priests founding the National Catholic Conference for

---

[19]Karen Johnson, "Beyond Parish Boundaries: Black Catholics and the Quest for Racial Justice," *Religion and American Culture* 25, no. 3 (Winter 2014): 264-300.

Interracial Justice structured the organization to maintain lay authority and refused to become a subsidiary of the bishop-led National Catholic Welfare Conference. By 1958, the aging LaFarge supported the national conference's independence from the bishops' official oversight.

The Catholic laity's increasing integration of faith and work contextualizes lay authors' support of Lewis. Noll shows that the lay-oriented periodicals contained more positive views about Lewis than priest-oriented periodicals, such as *American Ecclesiastical Review*. Charles Brady, the English professor whom Lewis praised as "the first of my critics so far who has really read and understood *all* of my books and 'made up' the subject in a way that makes you an authority," wrote authoritatively about Lewis. Brady published two articles in *America* in 1944, the same year LaFarge became the magazine's editor. The Jesuit-run periodical reached lay and priest readers alike and brought Catholic thinking from laypeople and priests to bear on current events. On the other hand, some priests still believed that priestly authority should trump lay experts and were particularly concerned about theological matters. Father Donnelly, for example, criticized lay reviewers for not warning Catholics away from Lewis because failure to do so was contrary to canon law.

THE INDIVIDUAL AND THE CHURCH

Significantly, even as laypeople integrated their faith with their work in the world, Catholics maintained a strong doctrine of the church. As Noll observes, the main negative response to Lewis's work suggested that he had a deficient understanding of the church. Laywoman Anne Fremantle and Father Harold Gardiner both critiqued Lewis's understanding of the church. As Fremantle wrote and Noll cites above, Lewis had a "a picayune view of the Church. . . . She, who is the Whole Christ, who in her body, and in that of each one of her members, completes the Passion." In this critique, Fremantle uses

Colossians 1:24 to highlight the corporate nature of the mystical body, in which each member has great value as they complete Christ's suffering. As members of Christ's body, Catholics were not simply autonomous individuals but called to submit to Christ even as they belonged to one another. This unity in Christ and embrace of suffering was central to interracialists' understanding of their work for racial justice and deserves exploration.

Fremantle refers to the effects of unity when she says that the church "completes the Passion." Catholics understood that their suffering could benefit other members of the body. Many Catholics— including those pursuing interracial justice—assumed that God did not call them to comfort. The demanding spiritual and relational work of loving people across racial lines required stepping into discomfort. Thomas Merton, one of Lewis's more famous reviewers, experienced this discomfort when he spent two weeks at Friendship House, a Catholic interracial settlement house in New York's African American Harlem community. Catherine de Hueck, an aristocratic refugee who fled the Russian Revolution, founded Friendship House. In 1938, Father John LaFarge, later the *America* magazine editor and one of Lewis's reviewers, influenced de Hueck's decision to come to Harlem and open a Friendship House branch. From Harlem, she asked White Catholics to join her in the work of interracial justice. Many White laypeople came. They met Black professionals, poets, and artists as well as poor residents. They provided meals, clothing, children's clubs, classes on African American history, and comfort as they were needed and able.[20] Merton visited Harlem's Friendship House in 1941 while trying to discern his vocation. This visit took

---

[20]Catherine De Hueck, "The Story of Friendship House," 1939 (box 1, folder 28, Ellen Tarry Papers, Schomburg Center for Research in Black Culture Archive); Al Schorsch, "'Uncommon Women and Others': Memoirs and Lessons from Radical Catholics at Friendship House," *U.S. Catholic Historian* 9, no. 4 (1990): 371-86; Elizabeth Louis Sharum, "A Strange Fire Burning: A History of the Friendship House Movement" (PhD diss., Texas Tech University, 1977); Johnson, *One in Christ*, 108-9, 118-24.

place after Merton reviewed Lewis's *Personal Heresy* and before he became a monk.

Conversation around the dinner table at Friendship House was rich, even if the fare was poor. Over watered-down soup shared with neighbors and visitors, Merton would likely have talked about the mystical body of Christ and the completion of Christ's passion through suffering. Discussion of these Catholic ideas would have been peppered with reference to bedbugs, voluntary poverty, and secondhand clothing. He probably contemplated his White identity in a Black context as well, which other White people considered. He would likely have eaten dinner with White Friendship House volunteer Ann Harrigan. Harrigan later lamented that her skin color made her an outsider when she founded a Friendship House branch in Chicago's Black Belt.[21] He may have heard Ellen Tarry, a famous Black children's author, read her stories to neighborhood children. Tarry may have shared what she often said, that White people should work *with* African Americans, not *for* them. If he had eyes to see, he may have observed how the White people at Friendship House too often failed to follow Tarry's advice.[22] But all the Catholics around the table—Black and White—would have known that their momentary struggles would bring healing to Christ's broken body, a body broken racially in the United States. Theirs was a robust understanding of the church.

PARTNERING WITH PROTESTANTS

Noll raises another important question concerning ecclesiology: Why were Catholics reading a lay Protestant writer as an authority on spiritual wisdom? Prior to the 1962–1965 reforms of the Second Vatican Council, Catholic doctrine understood the Catholic Church

---

[21]Johnson, *One in Christ*, 110.
[22]See Ellen Tarry, *The Third Door: The Autobiography of an American Negro Woman*, 2nd ed. (London: Staples, 1965), 144.

as *the* only way to Jesus. Part of Catholics' love for Lewis, Noll argues, is because Lewis and Catholic college graduates both valued classical training and natural law. Noll's treatment highlights another context that sheds light on this Catholic love of Lewis: the United States' identity shift from a Protestant to a "Judeo-Christian" nation.[23]

Scholars have debated the nature of the United States' religious identity. Religious diversity characterized North American history after contact: Native Americans had rich, varied spiritual lives, some of the earliest enslaved people were Muslim, and Catholics and different Protestant groups settled in different regions. Nonetheless, for three centuries Protestantism was the dominant religion. Protestantism's ascendance created a perennial question for Catholic Americans: Can one be both Catholic and American?

That question was particularly salient in the late nineteenth and early twentieth centuries because many immigrants were Catholic. In the 1880s, more immigrants from southeastern European countries came to the United States. Protestants assumed that because they were Catholic, they needed to be evangelized. Catholic immigrants' presence also prompted a crisis that reached its zenith in the 1920s among American-born "Anglo-Saxons." These White Americans were concerned that the immigrants would sully the "pure" bloodlines of those whom they saw as true Americans. In 1921 and 1924, Congress passed immigration laws severely limiting immigration. Because racial concerns were preeminent, they developed a quota system allowing immigrants from countries based on a ratio that matched the racial/ethnic makeup of the United States in 1880. The period also saw the rebirth of the Ku Klux Klan, whose members targeted Catholics for violence even more than African Americans. Catholic bishops responded with Americanization campaigns,

---

[23]Mark Silk, "Notes on the Judeo-Christian Tradition in America," *American Quarterly* 36, no. 1 (Spring 1984): 65-85; Kevin Schultz, *Tri-Faith America: How Catholics and Jews Held Postwar America to Its Protestant Promise* (New York: Oxford University Press, 2011).

limiting Catholic education in languages other than English and encouraging the faithful to assimilate.

In the 1930s, a subset of Catholics, Protestants, and Jews answered the question whether Catholics could be fully American with a resounding yes. In the context of increasing fascism and antisemitism internationally, Protestant, Catholic, and Jewish groups campaigned for broader inclusion in America. They argued that America was not a Protestant nation but a Judeo-Christian one. In a parallel development, many Catholic interracialists, aware of the magnitude of the problems they faced—and knowing that most African Americans were not Catholic—partnered with men and women outside the Catholic faith. Arthur Falls, the Black medical doctor and Catholic interracialist, worked closely with non-Catholics as a member of the Urban League, a Black racial uplift organization. As a Black Catholic, his experience with Protestants was not uncommon. But when he brought White Catholics to the Urban League meetings, it was often their first time engaging with non-Catholics in a substantial way.

During World War II, as the government tried to unite the nation behind a common cause, Americans increasingly identified as Judeo-Christian. By the 1950s, non-Catholics occupied key positions in Chicago's Catholic Interracial Council. Of course, not all people embraced the Judeo-Christian identity. As Noll shows, anti-Catholicism remained a factor in American life during the 1950s. However, liberal Protestants', Catholics', and Jews' efforts bore fruit nationally. While some criticized Americans' faith as vapid in the 1950s, a Judeo-Christian identity gave Americans a powerful way to distinguish themselves from "godless communism" during the Cold War.[24] When Soviet military leader Gregory Zhukov asked about the American religious foundation in 1954, Dwight Eisenhower struggled to explain it. He said, "Our form of government has no sense unless it is founded

---

[24]See, for instance, Will Herberg, *Protestant-Catholic-Jew* (Chicago: University of Chicago Press, 1983).

in a deeply felt religious faith, and I don't care what it is. With us, of course, it is the Judeo-Christian concept."[25] In 1960, John F. Kennedy, a Catholic, became president, further legitimizing the American Catholic identity. Even though Kennedy had to convince Protestants he would not take orders from the pope, his Catholicism did not preclude his becoming president.[26]

This sense of America as a Protestant, Catholic, and Jewish nation meant that each group saw the others as fully American. In this context, both Catholic priests and laypeople could praise a Protestant Christian author such as Lewis.

So where does this analysis leave us? It shows the racialized nature of the reviewers' lives, even if they were not thinking explicitly about race. It also emphasizes the importance of the doctrine of the mystical body of Christ both for advancing racial justice and for empowering laypeople to act *as Catholics* in their respective realms. The mystical-body doctrine is central to answering another significant question: What might people today learn *from* the Catholic reviewers and their generation? While the history I have narrated is somewhat recent, the people I discuss inhabited a very different world from our own. Those differences can help us see our own contexts more clearly.

Catholics' robust theology of an individual's corporate connection to others through Christ is striking. These Catholics' ecclesiology contrasts with the individualism that characterizes much of

---

[25]People have interpreted this statement in various ways, but a close reading of the text and context suggest that Eisenhower was not flippant with his statement but was assuming that religion was necessary for democracy. For our purposes, the president-elect conveyed an assumption about America: that it was Judeo-Christian. See Patrick Henry, "'And I Don't Care What It Is': The Tradition-History of a Civil Religion Proof-Text," *Journal of the American Academy of Religion* 49, no. 1 (March 1981): 35-49.

[26]Former Catholic Worker John Cogley helped Kennedy convince the American people he would work independently of the pope. Cogley had been one of the young White Catholics Arthur Falls drew into Catholic interracialism. See Cogley, *A Canterbury Tale* (New York: Seabury, 1976).

contemporary American life.[27] Catholics' emphasis on ontological unity—that people are united in a mystical way, even if unrealized in the present on earth—reminds me of the significance of Christians' unity in Christ. That unity is eternal. As Lewis wrote in *The Weight of Glory*, it "is immortals whom we joke with, work with, marry, snub, and exploit—immortal horrors or everlasting splendors."[28] That unity crosses the very significant barriers of race, even as it finds beauty in the unique experiences of different people.

To what extent are we living into that unity? Are we helping to create contexts where it is easier to be good? Easier to find God? Catholic laypeople in the Depression and World War II period tried to leaven the world with Jesus' love. They knew they needed one another. They believed that they were called to suffer with and for one another as they sought the fulfillment of God's kingdom on earth. May that be said of us in our generation.

---

[27]This individualism is particularly strong among White evangelicals. See Michael Emerson and Christian Smith, *Divided by Faith: Evangelical Religion and the Problem of Race in America* (New York: Oxford University Press, 2000).

[28]C. S. Lewis, "Learning in War-Time," in *The Weight of Glory and Other Addresses* (New York: HarperOne, 2001), 47-63.

"LIKE A FRESH WIND"

RECEPTION IN SECULAR
AND MAINSTREAM MEDIA

MARK A. NOLL

THE CAREFUL CRITICAL attention directed by Catholic reviewers to C. S. Lewis raises the natural question as to which other Americans joined them in finding Lewis an author to notice, discuss, and evaluate. As it happened, coverage in major newspapers such as the *New York Times*, popular magazines such as *Time*, and scholarly journals such as *Modern Language Notes* was just as interesting in what they wrote about Lewis as well as in what those responses tell us about the state of American culture as reflected in these newspapers and journals.

The secular media addressed the same seventeen works as Catholic reviewers but, as one would expect, with different interests.[1] For this broader range of periodicals, clear divisions marked assessments of his literary scholarship, responses to his imaginative works, and judgments about his Christian expositions. Before long these same sources also published general articles about Lewis and his work of the sort that continue to this day.

---

[1] For those works, see table 1 in the introduction.

AS LITERARY SCHOLAR

C. S. Lewis's first serious American reader engaged him on specifically Christian questions, and the first of his books reviewed by Americans, *The Pilgrim's Regress*, was an allegorical account of his Christian conversion. Yet into the early 1940s most who treated Lewis on this side of the Atlantic engaged with him primarily as a literary scholar. As an indication for how early attention to Lewis shed light on American public life, it is noteworthy that most of this literary assessment came from elite intellectual precincts—and that most of the critics from these precincts seemed comfortable with Lewis's respect for objective truth, general morality, and specifically Christian values.

Lewis's first American reader was Paul Elmer More, a classicist, journalist, and eccentric Christian apologist whom Lewis met at Oxford in 1933.[2] More, a student of Sanskrit, supporter of Irving Babbitt's "new humanism," and from 1918 a lecturer in classics at Princeton, hit it off with Lewis immediately. They exchanged complimentary letters about each other's writings—Lewis on More's *The Skeptical Approach to Religion*, which defended Christianity against its modernist interpreters, and More on Lewis's essay that first attacked E. M. W. Tillyard for "The Personal Heresy."[3] To be sure, they did disagree on important matters—Lewis defended Greek philosophical idealism as a possible way to the God of Christianity, which More disparaged, and More valued T. S. Eliot's work, which Lewis did not. Yet Lewis obviously found More's defense of Christian faith appealing as More set out that defense in a complex relationship to the main traditions of classical Western philosophy. More, however, passed away in 1937, only shortly after Lewis's books became available in America.

---

[2] Biographical details are supplied in Scott Michaelsen, "More, Paul Elmer," American National Biography online; and Byron C. Lambert, "The Regrettable Silence of Paul Elmer More," *Modern Age* 41 (Winter 1999): 47-54, with 52-53 on More and Lewis.

[3] C. S. Lewis to Paul Elmer More, October 25, 1934; April 5, 1935; May 23, 1935, in *Books, Broadcasts, and the War, 1931–1949*, vol. 2 of *The Collected Letters of C. S. Lewis*, ed. Walter Hooper (San Francisco: HarperSanFrancisco, 2004), 145-46, 156-58, 163-65.

Although Americans paid some attention to *The Pilgrim's Regress*, soon thereafter Lewis's *Allegory of Love*, an extensive tour of medieval and Renaissance love poetry, drew more and more serious attention from a number of leading American academics. In the *Journal of Modern History*, Roland Bainton of Yale Divinity School, who later published a landmark biography of Martin Luther, neatly summarized the burden of Lewis's *Allegory of Love*: "Edmund Spenser [in the *Faerie Queene*] is the pioneer in uniting the courtly tradition of the romance of unwedded love with the Christian standard of monogamy."[4] In *Speculum*, the nation's first journal devoted exclusively to medieval studies, Howard R. Patch of Smith College and a noted Chaucer expert conceded that Lewis afforded "excellent reading," but he objected to the book's "air of carelessness" and what he considered misreadings of Sir Thomas Malory and Geoffrey Chaucer.[5] Other prominent Chaucer scholars begged to differ. In an article on Chaucer's *Troilus and Criseyde*, one of the works Lewis treated in detail, Karl Young of the Yale English department credited Lewis as "the only critic" who caught Chaucer's true purpose.[6] Young's article appeared in *Publications of the Modern Language Association of America*, the journal of record for that well-regarded academic organization. Thomas A. Kirby, who would soon publish a full academic study of this one Chaucer work, called Lewis's treatment of courtly love poetry "the best general discussion of the subject available in English."[7] That review was published in *Modern*

---

[4]Roland Bainton, "Changing Ideas and Ideals in the Sixteenth Century," *Journal of Modern History* 8 (December 1936): 438.

[5]Howard R. Patch, review of *The Allegory of Love*, *Speculum* 12 (April 1937): 272-74.

[6]Karl Young, "Chaucer's 'Troilus and Criseyde' as Romance," *Publications of the Modern Language Association of America* 53 (March 1938): 40, with further commendation of Lewis's work on 41 and 46. Lewis and Young enjoyed a warm epistolary relationship; see C. S. Lewis to Karl Young, April 7, 1943; and the consoling letter to Young's widow, April 6, 1944, in Hooper, *Collected Letters* 2:567-68, 611.

[7]Thomas A. Kirby, review of *The Allegory of Love*, *Modern Language Notes* 52 (November 1937): 515-18, here 515. See Kirby, *Chaucer's Troilus: A Study in Courtly Love* (Baton Rouge: Louisiana State University Press, 1940).

Language Notes. And in the pages of *The American Historical Review*, Gray C. Boyce, a medievalist at Princeton, praised Lewis for being "as sane as he is sure, and very human."[8]

With attention from scholars at leading American universities and in a number of first-rank academic periodicals, Lewis's *Allegory of Love* gained scholarly respect for the author *before* he became widely known as a Christian apologist. The forthright Christianity of *The Pilgrim's Regress* did not become an issue (perhaps because the allegory displayed the same breadth of learning in classical, medieval, and Renaissance texts as the literary work). Lewis's sprightly prose also impressed most reviewers (Boyce in the *American Historical Review* loved that in a work of rarefied medieval scholarship Lewis referred, tellingly, to Mickey Mouse). The result was recognition that he had made a convincing case: Spenser's *Faerie Queene* was indeed, as Lewis wrote, "the greatest among the founders of that romantic conception of marriage which is the basis of all our love literature from Shakespeare to Meredith."[9] High academic standards supporting a literary argument that was not in the least preachy or apologetical yet defended one feature of Western Christian tradition—this resonated in an American environment that still made room for at least some aspects of that traditional culture.

And so it went with American responses to Lewis's other literary works, though R. D. Jameson of the Library of Congress did express a negative judgment about Lewis's collection of literary essays, *Rehabilitations*. According to Jameson, Lewis's effort to restore the reputation of selected English poets did provide "a pleasant summer

---

[8]Gray C. Boyce, review of *The Allegory of Love*, *American Historical Review* 43 (October 1937): 103-4. Another positive assessment, though with more reservations than Young, Kirby, or Boyce expressed, came from Edgar C. Knowlton, *Journal of English and Germanic Philology* 36 (January 1937): 124-26. Stanton A. Coblentz in the *New York Times Book Review* called the work a "percipient survey" (July 5, 1936, 12).

[9]C. S. Lewis, *The Allegory of Love* (Oxford: Clarendon, 1936), 360.

companion" but was "a dangerous guide" to the authors in question.[10] Opinions were more positive for *The Personal Heresy*, Lewis's debate with E. M. W. Tillyard on whether criticism of a poem should focus on the poet or the poet's subject matter. In 1936 Arthur O. Lovejoy of Johns Hopkins University had inaugurated an enduring tradition of American intellectual history with his book *The Great Chain of Being*. Four years later he cofounded *The Journal of the History of Ideas*, for which he supplied the first article in the journal's first issue. This article, "Reflections on the History of Ideas," included a strong commendation of *The Personal Heresy*, particularly the "argumentative verve and skill" with which Lewis lamented "the steadily increasing role of biography in our literary studies."[11] After Thomas Merton's review in the *New York Times*, which was treated in chapter one, Lovejoy's was the most extensive American commendation of this work.

American reviewers were even more enthusiastic about Lewis's *Preface to Paradise Lost*, which they noticed about the same time *The Screwtape Letters* burst on the American scene. These favorable reviews emphasized what Lewis himself stressed, that "Milton's thought, when purged of its theology, does not exist."[12] To Irene Samuel of Hunter College and a future president of the Milton Society, the book was "an excellent book to put into the hands of intelligent students."[13] William R. Parker, who later published a definitive biography of Milton, did wish that Lewis had noticed some of the scholarship produced by Americans but agreed with Lewis's plea "that

---

[10]R. D. Jameson, review of *Rehabilitations*, *Modern Language Notes* 55 (March 1940): 235-37, here 236.

[11]Arthur O. Lovejoy, "Reflections on the History of Ideas," *Journal of the History of Ideas* 2 (January 1940): 10. Lovejoy's associate at Johns Hopkins, philosopher George Boas, expressed a mixed opinion on this same work. See Boas, review of *The Personal Heresy*, *Modern Language Notes* 55 (March 1940): 233-34.

[12]C. S. Lewis, *A Preface to Paradise Lost* (Oxford: Oxford University Press, 1942), 64.

[13]Irene Samuel, review of *A Preface to Paradise Lost*, *Philosophical Review* 53 (November 1944): 589-90. For her biography, see Stella P. Revard, "Eulogy for Irene Samuel," *Milton Quarterly* 26 (October 1992): 94-96.

Figure 2.1. Along with several other well-placed American academics, Arthur O. Lovejoy spoke highly of the young C. S. Lewis's literary scholarship.

twentieth century readers make an effort to achieve seventeenth century attitudes, taking Milton as he [was] meant to be taken."[14] Edward Wagenknecht, a widely published scholar on literature and much else, wrote with particular reference to Lewis's insistence that Milton's Christian cosmology should always provide the starting point of criticism. His review in the *New York Times* ended by

[14]William R. Parker, review of *A Preface to Paradise Lost*, *Modern Language Notes* 59 (March 1944): 205-6. See Parker, *Milton: A Biography*, 2 vols. (Oxford: Clarendon, 1968), which ranks Lewis's study among "especially valuable" recent works on the poem (1113n33).

asserting that "with this book coming on the heels of 'The Screwtape Letters,' there is no longer any reason for failing to recognize that the defense of Christian culture did not end when Chesterton fell to the earth."[15]

As in Britain, so too in the United States, attention to Lewis's imaginative works and direct Christian expositions soon eclipsed considerations of his literary scholarship. Yet as enthusiasm for that later writing illuminates American popular culture, so also did the early reception of Lewis's literary scholarship shed light on the nation's intellectual culture.

It is first noteworthy that respect for Western Christian traditions and for philosophical realism remained alive despite the growing influence of John Dewey's morally relativistic pragmatism and the middlebrow vogue of Freudianism.

A second, related observation concerns fashions in literary criticism. Lewis shared several traits with what would soon be called "the New Criticism," a commitment to close readings and careful linguistic research. He stood, however, completely at odds with the new critics' dismissal of questions about truth claims or objective morality. Unlike the New Critics, Lewis also maintained that patient attention to the historical contexts of literary works paid rich dividends in understanding what those works were about. As American reviews commended Lewis's works, they revealed their substantial agreement with him on such questions. Only after the New Criticism ran its course would English departments agree with Lewis that universal moral standards mattered, but the moral standards dominating the more recent study of English concerned the exercise of economic, social, and gender-related power instead of standards from Western Christian heritage.

---

[15] Edward Wagenknecht, review of *A Preface to Paradise Lost*, *New York Times Book Review*, May 23, 1943, 10. On Wagenknecht, see the Boston University obituary, "Obituaries," *B.U. Bridge*, September 3, 2004, www.bu.edu/bridge/archive/2004/09-03/obituaries.html.

A third observation concerns the character of scholarship itself. Learning in the United States of the 1940s was not yet completely professionalized, as indicated by the respect in which academics held Paul Elmer More, Arthur O. Lovejoy, and Lewis himself, none of whom had earned a PhD. Although the accessible brilliance of Lewis's prose did set him apart, many learned Americans—such as More, Lovejoy, Edward Wagenknecht, and Roland Bainton—wrote books grounded in careful scholarship that they hoped would be read outside the academy.

Recognition of C. S. Lewis as a formidable literary scholar did not have an earthshaking effect on American intellectual life. This recognition did, however, reveal that during the era of World War II some American intellectuals valued at least some of what Lewis's scholarship also emphasized.

AS AUTHOR OF IMAGINATIVE WORKS

Earthshaking, however, is an appropriate word for the American reception of Lewis's popular writing. For his books of Christian exposition, reactions were more complicated, but for the imaginative works, the easy question to answer is: How did mainstream American media respond? Simple answer: with only a few qualifications, they loved these books, even loved them ecstatically. The more difficult question is: What did this overwhelmingly positive response say about American public culture as represented by the mainstream media?

In 1944 a contributor to the *Chicago Tribune* opined that for all the publicity lavished on the recently published *Screwtape Letters*, readers had made a mistake if they had overlooked *The Pilgrim's Regress*, which he called "a glorious dream story in the best Bunyan tradition" and possibly "Lewis' masterpiece." In this commendation, the *Tribune* only underscored what the *New York Times* had said in December 1935 after Sheed & Ward bought out the American edition of that allegory: "To those not convincedly materialistic in their outlook it will give new viewpoints. To many it will seem like a fresh wind blowing across arid wastes."[16]

About *The Screwtape Letters*, the *Times* expressed a more cautious judgment ("What the New World will think of it [in contrast to British enthusiasm] remains to be seen"). By contrast, in the *Saturday Review of Literature*, Leonard Bacon, who in 1941 had received the Pulitzer Prize for Poetry, did not hesitate: "This admirable, diverting, and remarkably original work . . . [is] the most exciting piece of Christian apologetics that has turned up in a long time."[17] Bacon's praise, rather than the *Times*'s equivocation, also characterized mentions of the book in the *Atlanta Constitution*, the *Los Angeles Times*, the *Chicago Tribute*, and the *Washington Post*.[18]

For Lewis's next fantasy, enthusiasm did not flag. Edward Wagenknecht, who had hailed *A Preface to Paradise Lost*, wrote in the *Chicago Tribune* that *The Great Divorce* did not quite come up to *The Screwtape Letters*, "that masterpiece." Yet Wagenknecht still thought this latest effort was superb: "If you have not yet discovered Mr. Lewis as the most challenging writer on religious themes that our generation has produced, I won't know where you could better begin to get acquainted with him than here."[19]

[16]Vincent Starrett, "Books Alive," *Chicago Daily Tribune*, April 2, 1944, E12; Jane Spence Southron, review of *The Pilgrim's Regress*, *New York Times Book Review*, December 8, 1935, 7.

[17]P. W. Wilson, review of *The Screwtape Letters*, *New York Times Book Review*, March 28, 1943, 3; Leonard Bacon, review of *The Screwtape Letters*, *Saturday Review*, April 17, 1943, 20. In a later *Times* review, P. W. Wilson speaks more highly of Lewis's radio broadcasts: P. W. Wilson, "The Man of Nazareth," *New York Times Book Review*, November 4, 1945, 6.

[18]Louie D. Newton, "Good Morning," *Atlanta Constitution*, March 3, 1943, 7; Paul Jordan Smith, "I'll Be Judge, You Be Jury," *Los Angeles Times*, March 7, 1943, C5; "Cathedral Book Club," *Chicago Daily Tribune*, October 19, 1943, 16; Dorothy Walworth, "Woman Treats Religion Well," *Washington Post*, March 17, 1946, S4.

[19]Edward Wagenknecht, review of *The Great Divorce*, *Chicago Daily Tribune*, March 17, 1946, G3.

Figure 2.2. This photograph of a young W. H. Auden would have been taken not long before he reviewed Lewis's *Great Divorce* in *The Saturday Review*.

A review of *The Great Divorce* in *The Saturday Review of Literature* provided one of the most intriguing of all American responses to Lewis in this period. According to W. H. Auden, who had relocated from Britain to the United States in 1939, it was "unlikely" that any other work published that year would be so "generally interesting" and "generally instructive." The year after Auden wrote his review of *The Great Divorce* he received the Pulitzer Prize for Poetry for a book-length poem, *The Age of Anxiety*, that gave the era a descriptor that has stuck. Auden did criticize Lewis's allegory for trying to imitate provincial dialects, for introducing a real-life figure (Napoleon), and for unnecessarily demeaning the reptile world by identifying lust with a lizard. His most interesting criticism, however, addressed Lewis's treatment of artists tempted by pride. For its shrewd analysis, which probably reflected Auden's own experience and with which Lewis, who repeatedly identified pride as the most basic human failing, would probably have agreed, Auden's criticism is worth quoting in full: "In [Lewis's] treatment of the sins which tempt the artist, he tries to combine in one figure two mutually exclusive idolatries: the pride from which some artists, usually the bad ones, suffer is of demanding public recognition; the pride of others, usually the good ones, is of not caring whether the public 'gets'" what the writer or painter hopes to convey. Critique notwithstanding, Auden's review ended by stressing "all the positive merits" of the work and by wishing that "those who, like myself, take delight in Mr. Lewis' writing" would also read Charles Williams, "a writer as unjustly ignored by American publishers as Mr. Lewis is widely and deservedly recognized."[20]

Although Auden's particularly discerning review of *The Great Divorce* delved more deeply than other assessments, his appreciation spoke for almost all treatments in the nation's mainstream press. For those who picked up these imaginative works, the result was predictably both enjoyment and edification.

Judgments about the Ransom Trilogy ranged somewhat more widely, with the main difference lying only between those who offered tempered approval and those who expressed all-out enthusiasm. Enthusiasm was mostly the word when Macmillan published an American edition of *Out of the Silent Planet* in September 1943— from the *Saturday Review of Literature* ("C. S. Lewis's Magnificent Fantasy"), the *New York Herald Tribune* ("excellent escape fiction as well as examination and criticism of modern life"), and the *Chicago*

---

[20]W. H. Auden, review of *The Great Divorce*, *Saturday Review*, April 13, 1946, 22-23.

Tribune ("a masterpiece"). Only the *New York Times* hesitated: while enjoying "the author's Miltonic love of light," its reviewer thought that the novel "lacks humor. Most Utopias do."[21]

Concerning *Perelandra*, the main New York reviewing papers liked it but only moderately. The *Herald Tribune* thought that the novel did not "quite come off," while the *Times* held that the story's "bare intellectual bones" made it read in spots like "a nocturnal argument conducted in the second year of theological school."[22] Other reviews were more positive. The *Christian Science Monitor* wrote that *Perelandra* "displays [Lewis's] great narrative and descriptive powers," and the *Chicago Tribune* that it is "a crystal clear well of thought." In the *Saturday Review of Literature*, Leonard Bacon once again pulled out all the stops. His assessment of *Perelandra* appeared in an issue with an image of Lewis on the cover (three and a half years before he graced the cover of *Time* magazine) along with a short statement about Lewis's "captivating myth." The review itself called Lewis "one of the most exciting and satisfactory writers who has come to the surface out of the maelstrom of these turbulent times."[23]

Although most reviews of *That Hideous Strength* judged it somewhat inferior to the two previous novels, this time a review in the *New York Times* led the chorus of praise: "The most eloquent, witty, learned, and altogether brilliant literary champion of the Christian religion now writing is . . . C. S. Lewis." The novel "is written with such fire and dash, such pace and skill that much of its peculiar symbolism goes down painlessly. . . . Its constant moralizing

---

[21]Ben Ray Redman, review of *Out of the Silent Planet, Saturday Review*, October 16, 1943, 52; Charles Neider, review, *New York Herald Tribune Weekly Book Review*, October 3, 1943, 12; Will Davison, review, *Chicago Tribune*, June 9, 1946, B11; Horace Reynolds, review, *New York Times Book Review*, October 3, 1943, 16.

[22]Maxwell Geismar, review of *Perelandra, New York Herald Tribune*, March 18, 1944, 9; Marjorie Farber, review, *New York Times Book Review*, March 26, 1944, 4.

[23]Harold Hobson, review of *Perelandra, Christian Science Monitor*, June 5, 1943, 11; Will Davidson, review, *Chicago Daily Tribune*, April 2, 1944, E11; Leonard Bacon, review, *Saturday Review*, April 8, 1944, 9.

is so honest, so penetrating in its understanding of men and society that it does not repel as didactic writing so often does in fiction."[24]

When thinking about what these responses to Lewis's allegories and his science fiction tell us about the American situation of the era, the most obvious point is probably the most important. These works of imaginative fiction received steady, widespread, and basically positive attention in the United States' most prominent print media, including book reviews in the national newspapers of record from New York City. Those who managed these media and those who wrote for them may have been surprised to find such lively works conveying such obvious Christian intentions. But once past the surprise, the media focused mostly on *how well* those works accomplished those intentions. The nation's public sphere may have been preoccupied with current events and may have left behind the instinctive Christian habits of earlier generations. Yet that public sphere could still respond positively to Christian writing when it was artfully framed.

A few reviewers did specify how Lewis's books spoke to the crises of the hour. Leonard Bacon, in his rave review of *The Screwtape Letters*, saw the book's "theology of hell" as exposing the follies of "Hitler's politics" and counteracting the message of the German Reich minister of propaganda, "Doctor [Joseph] Goebbels." A reviewer of *Out of the Silent Planet* wrote that arguments from the evil scientist Weston showed him keeping "one jump ahead of the Nazis." Another reviewer depicted the extended debates between Ransom and Weston in *Perelandra* as containing "many subtle analogies to the present struggle of our planet," presumably between Western liberty and Nazi tyranny.[25] Other reviews accounted

---

[24]Orville Prescott, review of *That Hideous Strength*, *New York Times*, May 21, 1946, 21. Interestingly, another review six weeks later in the *Times* is less positive: Theodore Spencer, review, July 7, 1946, 103.

[25]Leonard Bacon, review of *The Screwtape Letters*, *Saturday Review*, April 17, 1943, 20; Horace Reynolds, review of *Out of the Silent Planet*, *New York Times Book Review*, October 3, 1943, 16; Marjorie Farber, review of *Perelandra*, *New York Times Book Review*, March 26, 1944, 4.

for Lewis's effectiveness by pointing out how well he spoke to the intellectual questions "of our own day," how ably he countered fashionable educational theories that simply dismiss "old books," or how effectively he advanced "social criticism" through the medium of science fiction.[26] Several critics, in other words, accounted for Lewis's popularity by how skillfully he spoke to current events or about current intellectual fashions.

Mostly, however, the response to Lewis's imaginative works showed that gatekeepers for the nation's public media could celebrate skillful creative writing, even if that writing was chock-full of traditional Christian themes. In an important contrast to our own day, it is noteworthy that the Christian themes Lewis advanced had nothing to do with political polemics—neither for nor against Franklin Roosevelt's New Deal, neither defending nor questioning American involvement in World War II, neither praising nor condemning the great expansion of central government power occasioned by the New Deal and the war effort. Although Lewis may have had opinions on these matters, they did not shape his books in obvious ways.

So it was that reviewers time after time returned to the sparkle, the imaginative verve, and the unobtrusive brilliance of Lewis's work. Leonard Bacon's encomium in his treatment of *Perelandra* was unusual only in doubling down on what most other reviewers said: Lewis

> has a powerful, discriminating, and, in the proper sense of the
> word, poetic mind, startling wit, an overwhelming imagination,
> a charming and disarming naiveté, and the capacity to express
> himself best described by saying "He can write." . . . In so short
> a notice it has been impossible to give a notion of the freshness

---

[26]Jane Spencer Southron, review of *The Pilgrim's Regress*, *New York Times Book Review*, December 8, 1935, 7; Leonard Bacon, review of *The Screwtape Letters*, *Saturday Review*, April 17, 1943, 20; Charles Neider, review of *Out of the Silent Planet*, *New York Herald Tribune Weekly Book Review*, October 3, 1943, 12.

and clearness, the unpretentious nobility of the fable and the thought.[27]

Recognition of that sheer creative exuberance lies behind the many literary comparisons found in reviews. As with several of Lewis's Catholic readers, writers in the mainstream press also likened him to G. K. Chesterton.[28] The *New York Times*'s enthusiastic review of *That Hideous Strength* compared this book favorably to Aldous Huxley's *Brave New World* from 1932. But where Huxley in that famous story communicated "cynical despair," Lewis "as a devout Christian . . . [is] convinced that he knows the answer to the moral crisis of modern man."[29] A number of critics praised Lewis's space novels as worthy successors to the works of H. G. Wells, the first celebrated writer of science fiction in English. Americans would have especially resonated with that commendation because of how fresh their memory remained of a national sensation from only a few years before. In 1938, Orson Welles had produced a radio drama of H. G. Wells's tale *The War of the Worlds* that convinced many listeners of the reality of an ongoing invasion from Mars. To liken the author of *Out of the Silent Planet* or *Perelandra* to H. G. Wells was a compliment indeed.[30]

---

[27]Leonard Bacon, review of *Perelandra*, *Saturday Review*, April 8, 1944, 9.

[28]Wagenknecht, review of *A Preface to Paradise Lost*; Marjorie Farber, review of *Perelandra*, *New York Times Book Review*, March 26, 1944, 4 (Farber thought that Chesterton propounded his theology without, as she said about Lewis, jolting "the reader out of fantasy into the classroom").

[29]Orville Prescott, review of *That Hideous Strength*, *New York Times*, May 21, 1946, 21. Later that year, one of Chad Walsh's first of many essays on Lewis provided an extended comparison between these two authors, who, as many know, would die on the same day as the assassination of John F. Kennedy, November 22, 1963. See Chad Walsh, "Aldous Huxley and C. S. Lewis: Novelists of Two Religions," *Journal of Bible and Religion* 14 (August 1946): 139-43.

[30]The reviews of *Out of the Silent Planet* that appeared in the two New York City papers of record on the same day, October 3, 1943, both invoke Wells: Horace Reynolds, *New York Times Book Review*, 16; Charles Neider, *New York Herald Tribune Weekly Book Review*, 12. For other Wells-Lewis comparisons with *Perelandra* the focus, see Harold Hobson, *Christian Science Monitor*, June 5, 1943, 11; Marjorie Farber, *New York Times Book Review*, March 1944, 4.

In sum, mastery of the writer's craft, put creatively in service to ideas that enjoyed only a precarious hold on the educated public, could nonetheless gain a hearing for those ideas. From that conclusion came the surprising judgment from gatekeepers of the American mind that effective Christian allegory might not be an out-of-date relic of the past and that science fiction could deliver far more than simply a hypothetical view of the future.

CHRISTIAN EXPOSITION

Lewis's books of straightforward Christian exposition, along with *The Abolition of Man* and its refinement of arguments for an objective moral law, generated the era's widest range of critical opinion, though with positive responses still outnumbering the negative. Lewis's two key contentions in these works extrapolated the main motifs of his autobiographical allegory, *The Pilgrim's Regress*. First, human reasoning is impossible without acknowledging the instinctive human acceptance of objective moral principles. In other words, all humans everywhere have always sensed a fundamental difference between what they consider right and what they consider wrong. Second, the elements of traditional Christianity shared by most ecclesiastical traditions built naturally on this instinctive human conviction to provide a fleshed-out account of life in general and specific ethical ideals for life in the world. In other words, orthodox Christian faith provides exactly what humans long for once they realize that only divine revelation from beyond themselves can satisfy that longing. The mainstream media responded to both of these claims, though with less attention to Lewis on objective moral law than provided by Catholic reviewers and less concern for the details of Lewis's depiction of Christianity than offered by his Protestant reviewers. Still, coverage was extensive—and (perhaps surprisingly) positive.

In the eighteen months between September 1943 and March 1945, Macmillan published the three short books of Lewis's broadcast talks that in 1952 he would amalgamate as *Mere Christianity. The Case for Christianity* began by appealing to general human awareness of principles of right and wrong before sketching what Christians of all sorts believed, especially about the deity of Christ. *Christian Behaviour* described moral principles, including the classical "cardinal virtues," chastity outside marriage and fidelity within, and then hope and faith. As if anticipating W. H. Auden's later criticism of *The Great Divorce*, this book also devoted a chapter to the special danger of pride. *Beyond Personality* explained the Trinity, the timelessness of God, the Holy Spirit, the incarnation and resurrection of Christ, and the possibility of believers sharing the life of Christ. Unlike several reviewers of Lewis's imaginative works, responses to the three expository volumes did not invoke the world war as a context for Lewis's arguments.

One of the first reviews of *The Case for Christianity* appeared in the *New York Herald Tribune* from John Haynes Holmes, an indefatigable Unitarian reformer who helped found both the National Association for the Advancement of Colored People and the American Civil Liberties Union. Haynes praised Lewis for his clear depiction of natural law but then scored the book's second half for "an almost incredibly naïve statement of Christian theology." Yet two years later, for the same paper, Haynes had nothing but praise for *Beyond Personality*, a work marked by "clarity of thought," "simplicity of expression," and "a magic . . . which makes plain the most abstruse problems of theological speculation."[31]

A reviewer of *Beyond Personality* in an academic journal, ironically titled *The Personalist*, did mock Lewis by paraphrasing his presentation of Christianity as, "You can't understand it, so you take it upon the authority of one who reports what *the* Christian view is." But

---

[31]John Haynes Holmes, review of *The Case for Christianity, New York Herald Tribune Weekly Book Review*, November 14, 1943, 42; Holmes, review of *Beyond Personality, New York Herald Tribune Weekly Book Review*, September 23, 1945, 12.

other reviews of these works sang a different tune. To the *New York Times*, *Christian Behaviour* was "full of searching, kindly and shrewd observations. . . . Altogether a highly intelligent little religious book far bigger than its size." The *Times* offered a similar judgment on *Beyond Personality* by saying its "pages are crowded as ever with apt illustration, humorous ways of putting things—and searching rejoinders to negative plausibilities." A professor from the University of North Carolina echoed that judgment in the academic journal *Social Forces*: "*Christian Behavior* [sic] is a very practical and very modern application of Christian principles adopted to broadcast talks." One of several reviews of Lewis's books in the *Theosophical Forum* chimed in by describing this same book as "the clear, original, and sincere thoughts of one to whom Christianity is evidently a living way of vital experience."[32]

This positive review in the *Theosophical Review*, along with the same journal's later commendations of *The Screwtape Letters* and *The Great Divorce*, should be of particular interest for students of C. S. Lewis. Theosophy emerged in the late nineteenth century from the teaching of Helena Blavatsky as a form of esoteric Neoplatonism heavily influenced by Eastern religions. As it happens, Owen Barfield, a prolific author, creative linguist, and one of C. S. Lewis's lifelong closest friends as well as his solicitor, was influenced by a variation of Theosophy propounded by Rudolf Steiner, an Austrian whose variation became known as Anthroposophy. It is not clear, however, whether Barfield would have agreed with the reviewer who wrote, "A Theosophist would express [Lewis's] fundamentally sound ideas somewhat differently. . . . The phraseology expressing the idea of God is what an occultist would use in speaking of the Spiritual Monad

---

[32]I. G. Whitchurch, review of *Beyond Personality*, *The Personalist* 27 (1946): 334-35; Henry James Forman, review of *Christian Behaviour*, *New York Times Book Review*, April 23, 1944, 12; P. W. Wilson, review of *Beyond Personality*, *New York Times*, July 22, 1945, 98; Ernest R. Groves, review of *Christian Behaviour*, *Social Forces* 25 (December 1946): 223; L. W. Hart, review of *Beyond Personality*, *Theosophical Forum* 24 (March 1946): 3-4.

or the Higher Self, through which alone the composite being, man, can reach toward the Unknowable."[33]

For Lewis's directly Christian writing, University of Chicago philosopher Charles Hartshorne offered the longest and most searching response. By the time of his essay review in July 1944, Hartshorne had become well known as an earnest defender of theism, but of theism adjusted to notions of change, freedom, and contingency associated with the process philosophy of Alfred North Whitehead. Hartshorne's article in the journal *Ethics* asserted that Lewis's "case for theism is . . . quite unnecessarily compromised by the author's orthodoxy." In Hartshorne's opinion, contemporaries such as Lewis who "expound the [Christian] system from the inside should avoid cluttering up their accounts with bits of logical sophistication inherited from former ages." Hartshorne did concede that Lewis's defense of "traditional doctrine" was "more penetrating than most secular discussions." But he insisted that instead of a binary choice between atheistic naturalism and traditional Christian orthodoxy, the "Fechnarian-Schellingen-Whiteheadian doctrine," that is, "the panentheistic alternative," offered a better explanation for existence. According to Hartshorne, God did not stand outside the flux of life but existed within as a changing force unfolding God's own potential as the history of the universe and of humankind itself unfolded.[34] These comments on Lewis heralded a shift in general intellectual climate that requires more comment after we examine other reviews of his specifically Christian works.

In April 1947, Macmillan made Lewis's *The Abolition of Man* available to Americans, a work that had been published four years earlier in

---

[33]Hart, review of *Beyond Personality*, 4. See also K. Heck, review of *The Screwtape Letters*, *Theosophical Forum* 22 (July 1944): 332-33; and review of *The Great Divorce*, *Theosophical Forum* 24 (December 1946): 624. For a book appearing in the Wade Center's Hansen Lectureship Series, it is relevant to note that the headquarters of the American branch of the Theosophical Society is located in Wheaton, only a mile or so north of Wheaton College.

[34]Charles Hartshorne, "Philosophy and Orthodoxy" (essay review of *The Problem of Pain* and *The Case for Christianity*), *Ethics* 54 (July 1944): 295-98.

Britain. These published lectures do not present Christian doctrine as such, but they do make the same defense of objective moral law found in the Christian works, this time applied to modern theories of education—in particular, theories such as those of American pragmatist John Dewey, who concentrated on the practical effects of current actions while dispensing with any appeal to universally valid moral principles. Lewis's American reviewers obviously thought he was on to something important. The review in the *New York Herald Tribune* is noteworthy because it comes from Chad Walsh, who would soon be recognized as the nation's leading Lewis scholar. Walsh did ask whether Lewis may have underestimated the difference between moral codes from different times and places; he thought that "a vast qualitative difference lay between Aristotle's tranquil acceptance of slavery and Christ's teaching about our 'neighbor.'" Yet Walsh agreed that if the newer ideologies prevailed, "In place of man as we have known him there emerges a creature ruled by sheer subjectivism." George Stephenson in the *New York Times* claimed that Lewis was successfully defending the reality of "the Tao, Natural Law, First Principles. . . . He uses all the power of his sober analysis, keen wit, and logical reasoning to make his hearers and readers know that the casual dismissal of objective value will work untold harm in future generations."[35]

In *Miracles*, Lewis's next book published in America, he joined specifically Christian reasoning to his defense of natural law. Not surprisingly, Chad Walsh once again commended the result, on this occasion for the *New York Times*. As he put it, Lewis "is out to topple the whole imposing structure of naturalism, and to this reviewer's mind he does just that," with particularly effective treatment of "the grand miracle," the incarnation of Christ.[36]

---

[35]Chad Walsh, review of *The Abolition of Man*, *New York Herald Tribune Weekly Book Review*, April 13, 1947, 5; George R. Stephenson, review of *The Abolition of Man*, *New York Times Book Review*, May 18, 1947, 22.

[36]Chad Walsh, review of *Miracles*, *New York Times Book Review*, September 28, 1947, 5, 34.

Figure 2.3. This image shows Chad Walsh of Beloit College at about the age when he published some of the earliest and most perceptive reviews of Lewis's work—and in both religious and general periodicals.

Max Carl Otto, chairman of the University of Wisconsin's philosophy department, took a very different view of *Miracles* in an essay that, like Charles Hartshorne's, subjected Lewis to intense philosophical scrutiny. Otto, who over the course of a respected philosophical career moved from the confessional Lutheranism of his parents to defending a nontheistic view of nature and humanity, complained that Lewis practiced "obscurantism" by not heeding contemporary scholarship on the New Testament. (Lewis in a later lecture responded to such criticism as Dorothy L. Sayers did when she mocked "the assured results" of such modern scholarship with her own "higher criticism" of the Sherlock Holmes stories.)[37] Again, however, with almost all who disagreed with Lewis, Otto commended his "lucid and fresh . . . style, enlivened by an abundance of colorful metaphors." Yet Otto's commitment to naturalism ruled out the possibility of miracles, which Lewis argued for from experience. According to this critic, Lewis's failure to recognize "present-day intellectual and social actualities" doomed what he wanted to say in favor of supernaturalism.[38]

Although Otto's review reflected a great deal of philosophical learning, except in one point it did not really engage Lewis's argument about the self-defeating character of philosophical naturalism. (If all thought arises only from physical causes, then the concluding thought that "all human reason is explained by physical causes" reflects only the interaction of atoms with no claim to describing the world as it really is. In a variation on Lewis's argument more than half a century later, Alvin Plantinga called the theory of naturalistic evolution a "self-defeater" for claiming to derive a universal truth from physical processes incapable of asserting any claims about universal truths.)[39] The one point where Otto did engage Lewis's arguments concerned the claim that atheistic

---

[37]C. S. Lewis, "Modern Theology and Biblical Criticism," in *Christian Reflections*, ed. Walter Hooper (Grand Rapids: Eerdmans, 1967), 152-66. As examples, see Dorothy L. Sayers, "Holmes' College Career," and "The Dates in *The Red-Headed League*," in Sayers, *Unpopular Opinions* (London: Victor Gollanz, 1946), 134-47, 168-78.

[38]M. C. Otto, review of *Miracles*, *Crozer Quarterly* 25 (January 1947): 61-64.

[39]Alvin Plantinga, *Where the Conflict Really Lies: Science, Religion, and Naturalism* (New York: Oxford University Press, 2011).

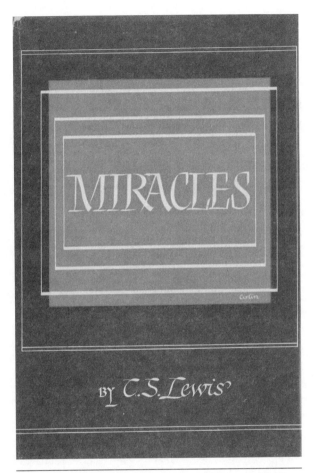

Figure 2.4. C. S. Lewis's *Miracles* received a warm American welcome, except from reviewers like Professor Max Carl Otto of the University of Wisconsin who had ruled out the possibility of the supernatural.

naturalism was "irrational." Otto contended that Lewis's argument represented a "willful refusal . . . to understand" what philosophical naturalists actually claimed.[40] In 1948, Catholic Oxford philosopher Elizabeth Anscombe made a similar complaint, which prompted

---

[40]Otto, review of *Miracles*, 63.

Lewis to make a small revision in later editions of *Miracles* that accepted Anscombe's distinction between the invalidity of "irrational" arguments and the potential validity of "nonrational" arguments within their own sphere of discourse.[41]

That kind of detailed argument is best left to professional philosophers. For more general purposes, the lengthy reviews of Lewis's work by Charles Hartshorne, an advocate of process philosophy, and Max Otto, an advocate of philosophical naturalism, revealed something important about the intellectual climate in which Lewis was being read. Otto's criticism pointed backward. It engaged Lewis on terrain he covered many times, an intellectual battlefield where the combatants took for granted that they were competing to discover *a single truth* about humankind and the world. The debate focused on where that truth would come from—from following science, from first ruling out the possibility of divine revelation, or (as with Lewis) from appealing to universal moral perceptions. For much of the reading public to our day, straightforward competing claims about *the truth* have remained very important, as indicated by the ongoing popularity of Lewis's book *Mere Christianity*. Its arguments about discerning *the truth* have obviously remained persuasive for many on its original terms.

By contrast, Hartshorne's essay—as well as the relativistic educational schemes Lewis attacked in *The Abolition of Man*—suggested that the philosophical universe in which Lewis came to faith and which he exploited to advance his Christian convictions was under assault. Hartshorne suggested that God, as the source of life, hope, and truth, *changed* in response to developments in the universe. Educational pragmatists dispensed with notions of universal truth entirely. Both anticipated claims about the situated character of all

---

[41]For a discerning account of Anscombe's life, including her response to C. S. Lewis, see Eric Wiland, "Gertrude Elizabeth Margaret Anscombe," *Stanford Encyclopedia of Philosophy*, May 30, 2022, https://plato.stanford.edu/entries/anscombe/#Lif.

knowledge that within a generation or slightly more would lead some influential thinkers to speak about conditions of postmodernity replacing the convictions of Enlightenment modernity. These later claims would explain the relative character of supposed truth as arising from the unequal exercise of power or from some other this-worldly force. These claims have been naturalistic like Otto's arguments, but they have contended for a fluid understanding of truth like Hartshorne's.

Yet in the decade surrounding World War II, the traditional expectation that serious thinking and research would reveal a single truth continued for the most part to prevail. Significantly, the matters that most concerned Catholic and Protestant readers responding to Lewis also remained important to critics writing for secular publications. Pathways between the upper regions of American intellectual culture and the American Christian churches were still wide open.

GENERAL ASSESSMENTS

Writers for American mainstream media were not as quick as Catholic authors such as Charles Brady to offer full assessments of Lewis's work, nor when they appeared were they anywhere near as thorough. Such assessments, however, did begin before the end of the war and have (of course) continued to the present day. About the character of American public life at the time, the general accounts show that a receptive but not unanimous audience remained open to traditional Christian writing, particularly if that writing was fresh, compelling, and unusually creative.

Alistair Cooke would soon gain appreciative listeners worldwide for his fifteen-minute weekly radio broadcasts on the BBC, *Letter from America,* and even more cachet when in 1971 he became the host of Public Television's *Masterpiece Theater.* For our purposes, however, he was noteworthy for publishing the first unreservedly dismissive report on Lewis for an American audience. It appeared in April 1944, shortly after Macmillan brought out American editions of *Christian Behaviour* and *Perelandra*. Cooke wrote it for *The New Republic*, a progressive weekly known for its edgy commentary on current politics and its soft spot for the Soviet Union. Cooke, perhaps reflecting his own rejection of the strict Protestantism in which he was raised and his involvement with a smart set at Cambridge, where he studied English, opined that times of war regularly "spawn[ed] quack religions and Messiahs." The article leaves no doubt that in his mind "the alarming vogue of Mr. C. S. Lewis" belonged in the quack category. According to Cooke, Lewis exploited the "doubting times" to become "a minor prophet, pressed into making a career of reassurance." In an interesting charge for someone who would soon become renowned for his own resonant radio broadcasts, Cooke complained that both on the air and in his books Lewis offered only "fantasies," "befuddlement," and "a patness that murders the issues it pretends to clarify." Cooke took particular offense at Lewis's defense of traditional views of "sex and marriage" as reflecting a "frightened dualism."[42]

The only other American publication in this era to attempt such a complete takedown was *The American Freeman*, a socialist-atheistical journal. Its December 1947 number ran an article by Victor S. Yarros, a collaborator with Clarence Darrow and a well-known anarchist, who slammed Lewis as a "pious paradox-monger and audacious word-juggler" whose "fundamentalism is no improvement on that of our Jehovah's Witnesses or of the Christian Scientists." To Yarrow, who like Cooke was heavy on invective but light on analysis, Lewis provided only "rubbish from any honest and sane point of view."[43]

---

[42]Alistair Cooke, "Mr. Anthony at Oxford," *New Republic*, April 24, 1944, 578-80.

[43]Victor S. Yarrow, "An Invitation to Rough Debunking," *American Freeman*, no. 2103 (December 1947): 4.

Journals both closer to the center of American opinion and with far larger circulations than *The New Republic* and *The American Freeman* contributed the other comprehensive assessments in these years. Chad Walsh, an Episcopalian who taught English at Beloit College in Wisconsin, read *Perelandra* with appreciation and then began a correspondence with Lewis.[44] In September 1946 the *Atlantic Monthly*, a respected magazine out of Boston, then in its eighty-ninth year, published his article, "C. S. Lewis: Apostle to the Skeptics." Its message was nicely summarized by the article's heading: "Here is the audacious story of what an Oxford don has done in his crusade against religious skepticism in the modern world." Walsh reported not quite accurately that Lewis "seems to have escaped the attention of most professional critics" before summarizing the commendations others offered piecemeal:

> Lewis writes as a layman to laymen. . . . He expresses himself with true Oxford urbanity. He has a sense of humor. (Since the death of G. K. Chesterton it has been generally assumed that no Christian apologist ever laughs.) Finally he has not confined himself to the straightforward, frontal attack. He has more than one weapon in his armory.

Walsh then enumerated those weapons as *The Screwtape Letters*, in a class by itself; the straightforward Christian exposition found in the three small books of broadcast talks and *The Problem of Pain*; "the interplanetary novels"; and finally Lewis's revival of "older literary forms" in *The Pilgrim's Regress* and *The Great Divorce*.

The lengthy article continued without considering Lewis's literary criticism, but with a careful unpacking of his traditional theological convictions and an argument about his importance as "one of the few Christian apologists who can both write simply and at the same time

---

[44]On the Lewis-Walsh friendship, see Walter Hooper, *C. S. Lewis: A Complete Guide to His Life and Works* (San Francisco: HarperSanFrancisco, 1996), 739-40. For Lewis's letter to Walsh in this period, see Lewis to Walsh, December 18, 1945, in Hooper, *Collected Letters* 2:686; there were many more letters from 1948 onwards.

avoid infuriating the more sophisticated readers by a pulpit vocabulary or the Sunday school flavor of piety." After mentioning
Dorothy L. Sayers as "his most popular rival," the article concluded
by prophesying that "if Christianity revives in England and America,
the odds are that it may bear strong traces of the Gospel according to
C. S. Lewis."[45] Encouraged by his wife, Eva, and after visiting Lewis at
Oxford in the summer of 1948, Walsh expanded this article into a 1949
book with the same title as the *Atlantic Monthly* article. Walter
Hooper later described it as "the first book about Lewis, and . . . one
of the best."[46]

Time magazine, cofounded by Henry Luce shortly after the First
World War, had become by the 1940s the nation's bestselling news
weekly. It was known for its worldwide coverage but also its quasi-
sensationalistic fascination with celebrities, sports, and Hollywood.
Time began reviewing Lewis in April 1943 with a favorable notice of
The Screwtape Letters, followed by short, positive reviews of *Christian
Behaviour* (January 1944), *The Great Divorce* (March 1946), and *That
Hideous Strength* (June 1946) and an article on George MacDonald
(June 1947).[47] A typical paragraph in *Time*'s review of *Christian
Behaviour* illustrates the jaunty, near-insouciance sought by the mag-
azine in all of its writing:

> Reluctant Believer. Red-cheeked, balding, Belfast-born, Clive
> Staples Lewis, 45, has been tutor and lecturer at Oxford's
> Magdalen College since 1925, teaches medieval English liter-
> ature. His lectures are an Oxford rarity: they are jampacked.

---

[45]Chad Walsh, "C. S. Lewis, Apostle to the Skeptics," *Atlantic Monthly* (September 1946):
115-19. Walsh's assessment was given wider currency when this article was abridged
under the same title in *The Religious Digest* 20 (May 1947): 11-14.

[46]Hooper, *C. S. Lewis: A Complete Guide*, 739.

[47]All of the *Time* articles are anonymous: "Sermons in Reverse" (*Screwtape Letters*), April
19, 1943, 78; "Little Hm" (*Out of the Silent Planet*), October 11, 1943, 102; "From Hell to
Heaven" (*Christian Behaviour*), January 24, 1944, 96; "Excursion from Hell" (*Great
Divorce*), March 11, 1946, 48; "Theological Thriller" (*That Hideous Strength*), June 10, 1946,
54; "Scottish Sage" (George MacDonald), June 2, 1947, 81.

During World War I he served in France with the Somerset Light Infantry, was invalided home. His aunt, says he, was relieved to learn that the wound in his back came from a misdirected British shell, and was not an indication that he had been running away from the Germans.

For its issue of September 8, 1947, Lewis's portrait joined the roster of world and American notables that had appeared on the magazine's covers since its founding. The issue's lengthy word-portrait described Lewis as "one of the most influential spokesmen for Christianity in the English-speaking world." It called him a latter-day G. K. Chesterton who, with other "literary evangelists (T. S. Eliot, Graham Greene, Dorothy Sayers, et al.)," was fueling "the new surge of curiosity about Christianity." It offered a brief commendation of Lewis's recently published book, *Miracles*, "a strictly unorthodox presentation of strict orthodoxy," before providing a sketch of Lewis's life that included his debt to George MacDonald, an account of his conversion, the success of his radio broadcasts, and a brief review of his other works from *The Pilgrim's Regress* to *The Great Divorce*. The article quoted an unnamed Briton who, while esteeming Lewis's literary work, thought he had turned to the "cheap sophism" of his directly Christian writing for the money. Appreciation, however, was the dominant note in *Time's* portrait of Lewis as "one of a growing number of heretics among modern intellectuals, an intellectual who believes in God."[48]

For the United States' mainstream secular culture by the late 1940s, *Time* magazine had become the equivalent of the Catholic bishops in guarding the faithful against ideas that lacked Henry Luce's *nihil obstat* and *imprimatur*—"nothing objectionable, and therefore allowed." Luce, cofounder and publisher of *Time*, was said to exert more influence on public opinion than even President

---

[48]"Don v. Devil," *Time*, September 8, 1947, 67-72.

Truman. Yet if the *Time* cover was not enough, shortly thereafter the West Coast press reported a startling story concerning Luce's wife, the glamorous and brilliant Clare Boothe Luce. This Luce, after gaining fame as an editor of *Vanity Fair*, a playwright, a member of Congress, a source of unending gossip about her love affairs, and a fixture in the annual list of most admired American women, had recently made a well-publicized conversion to Catholic Christianity. In late 1947 it was now reported that Mrs. Luce had been hired to transform *The Screwtape Letters* into a script to be filmed by the legendary Darryl Zanuck of Twentieth Century Fox. Luce explained that a screen adaptation of Lewis's work "could be an enormous force for good."[49] If, as it happened, nothing came of this venture (Luce's script fell flat, while Zanuck never got the point of the book), it did indicate how prominent C. S. Lewis had become in the arenas monitored by popular American media.

In a wider view, that popularity underscored the way that the public sphere in this earlier American era both resembled and differed from what came later in the nation's history. It was in many ways still a late Christian culture, though with mounting competition from pragmatism in educational theory, Freudianism in psychology, scientism in pop philosophy, and perhaps most of all from a war-inspired civil religion that retained God talk but not much actual Christianity. The secular gatekeepers of that culture marveled at Lewis's imaginative creativity and his ability to effortlessly communicate foundational truths of Christianity in language persuasive for the general public as well as for scholars. Some, such as Chad Walsh and Clare Boothe Luce, went beyond marveling to endorsing.

---

[49]Philip K. Scheuer, "Clare Boothe Luce Will Battle Devil in Hollywood," *Los Angeles Times*, December 7, 1947, B1. For this celebrity's efforts to make the movie, see Sylvia Jukes Morris, *Price of Fame: The Honorable Clare Booth Luce* (New York: Random House, 2015), 200-206.

RESPONSE

KIRK D. FARNEY

As Mark Noll demonstrates, commentators within the American academy and the mainstream media, notwithstanding certain vocal critics, found much to like in Lewis's literary output. While I find the academic receptivity, especially beyond Lewis's work as a literary scholar, to be particularly noteworthy, I would like to focus my remarks on the mainstream media response. The openness to, the respect for, the affinity toward, and even the endorsement of Lewis's work, with its sometimes subtle and often not-so-subtle Christian themes, invite further exploration. Such reaction from writers and editors within the mainstream media reflects, I believe, not only something about the mindset of these cultural contributors but also something about their perceptions of their readers' mindsets. Thus, we gain a greater understanding of American culture in the 1930s and 1940s.

It is not hard to understand why C. S. Lewis's creativity, wit, narrative craftsmanship, and apologetic adeptness generated appeal, across genres, with reviewers and readers. That the reception of his publications was "earthshaking," as mainstream media "loved them ecstatically," to use Noll's characterization, tells us that something in addition to good writing obviously was going on here. As mentioned, *Chicago Tribune* columnist Edward Wagenknecht refers to Lewis as "the most challenging writer on religious themes that our generation has produced." That is what must be understood about Lewis's appeal and the cultural atmosphere into which he spoke. During these decades, a vast number of Americans wanted their minds challenged, and in many cases their souls stirred, on matters relating to religious truth claims, especially those of a Christian variety. While perspectival divides existed between modernists and fundamentalists, Protestants and Catholics, and scoffers and saints, the quest for truth—capital-*T* Truth—by ordinary people was downright robust. In a period in which calamities and potential calamities (the Great Depression, World War II, and the commencement of the Cold War) created the "age of anxiety," Americans wanted something into which they could place their trust, and many were not opposed to that coming from religious sources.

I intend to reinforce this assessment by sharing some of my own research from this era, which might hint that, if anything, the meaning of Lewis's reception in the States is understated. I have spent a number of years researching the background, careers, homiletic content, and cultural impact of two "earthshaking" network radio preachers during the 1930s and 1940s—Walter A. Maier of *The Lutheran Hour* and Fulton J. Sheen of *The Catholic Hour.* Each week, these two purveyors of divine wisdom broadcast their messages coast to coast, via Mutual Broadcasting System and NBC microphones, respectively, to receptive ethereal congregants. And make no mistake, their preaching, albeit eloquent and inspiring, was challenging in remarkable ways. Each week millions of listeners tuned in to hear anything but dumbed-down or feel-good religion. If C. S. Lewis was the "most challenging writer on religious themes" of the generation, Sheen and Maier were arguably the most challenging *speakers* on religious themes of that generation.

Before I expound on this more completely, perhaps a word or two on who Walter Maier and Fulton Sheen were is in order. Born in Boston in 1893, to a middle-class German immigrant couple, Maier was educated at Concordia Collegiate Institute in Bronxville (New York), Boston University, and Concordia Seminary in St. Louis. Maier was ordained in the Lutheran Church–Missouri Synod in 1917. While a doctoral student at Harvard, he was surprised by an offer of a full professorship in Old Testament at Concordia Seminary, which he accepted. In 1929, Harvard granted him a PhD in Semitics, which required a working knowledge of ten languages, not counting those of European origin that he previously had mastered, such as German. In addition to his faculty duties at the seminary, Maier was the driving force in establishing the first Lutheran radio station in the country, KFUO, in 1924, and the launch of the nationally broadcast *The Lutheran Hour* in 1930. He served as *The Lutheran Hour* speaker from its inception to his untimely death at age fifty-six in 1950. At the time of his passing, Maier's weekly radio audience was estimated at twenty million, as his program was broadcast by over twelve hundred stations globally, reaching listeners in 120 countries, making him the most widely heard sermonizer in the world.

Fulton Sheen was born in 1895 in El Paso, Illinois, the son of middle-class, second-generation Irish immigrants. Educated in Catholic grade and high schools, Sheen went on to earn degrees at St. Viator's College in Bourbonnais, Illinois, St. Paul Seminary in Minnesota, and the Catholic University of America. Ordained into the priesthood in 1919, Sheen proceeded from the Catholic University of America to the University of Louvain, the leading European center for Thomistic studies. He completed his PhD in philosophy in 1923 and was invited to pursue the highly selective postdoctoral agrégé en philosophie, which he completed with "high distinction" in 1925. After a brief assignment as a curate in Peoria, Illinois, Sheen accepted a faculty position in the philosophy department of the Catholic University of America, where he taught for the next twenty-five years. When NBC radio offered a weekly network time slot to the Catholic Church for religious broadcasts in 1930, Sheen became the most prominent speaker on the program and remained so until he left in 1952 to begin his *Life Is Worth Living* weekly network television program. Sheen's weekly audience on *The Catholic Hour* was estimated to be as high as

17.5 million, with over 125 domestic stations broadcasting the program at the time of his radio departure. Listeners also tuned in via shortwave broadcasts that could be heard in North and South America, Europe, parts of Africa, Hawaii, and the Philippines.

When Maier and Sheen took to the airwaves in 1930, it was far from certain that their broadcasts would attract many listeners. These two highly educated clerics set out to preach objective, enduring, divine truth at a time when many perceived such ideas as having fallen out of fashion in the face of modernist skepticism, scientific advances, trending pragmatism, and loosening societal strictures. Yet the response that *The Lutheran Hour* and *The Catholic Hour* generated week after week tells us that millions of Americans shared their concerns about the lubricious state of truth. The embrace of C. S. Lewis's expositions on truth in various genres during this same period seems to be another manifestation of this mindset. In other words, the traditional narrative that at about this time a subset of the citizenry retreated into fundamentalist citadels while the rest of the populace simply accepted skeptical modernist viewpoints is entirely too simplistic. So is the explanation of a sweeping religious depression during this era as put forward by historian Robert Handy.[1]

Near the beginning of his radio ministry, Sheen fretted that "temporalism" had displaced eternal perspectives in too many quarters. Even religion, he noted, "has drunk deep of the intoxicating draughts of temporalism, and [is] now reeling under its effects." Modern philosophy "has become so obsessed with the notion that it teaches with unbuttoned pride that there is no such thing as Truth with a capital 'T,' for Truth is ambulatory: we make it as we go; it depends on the Time in which we live."[2] As Maier commenced his radio preaching, he

---

[1] Robert T. Handy, "The American Religious Depression, 1925–1935," *Church History* 29, no. 1 (March 1960): 3-16.
[2] Fulton J. Sheen, *Moods and Truths: How to Solve the Problems of Modern Living* (New York: Popular Library, 1956), 121-22.

observed that when the present "restless, disillusioned world echoes [Pontius Pilate's query of Jesus], 'What is truth,' people often ask the question with a calculated seriousness that is born of distrust and suspicion." A few sermons later, he lamented, "There is a haze of doubt and uncertainty that rises from . . . the smokescreen of modernist delusion by which the verities of our faith disappear into the black barrage of human speculation." Maier observed that "our modern, grasping, skeptical age" had come to rely solely on "human reason"—the "cold, calculating" and deeply flawed reason that it had unwisely "enthroned."[3] Capital-*T* Truth was in peril.

Maier and Sheen were not bashful about calling out various culprits in this regrettable state of affairs. They were particularly displeased, however, with modernist skeptics within the church itself. In the unsettling times in which they ministered, just when they were certain that the church should be doubling down on the immutable nature of its truth claims, these ecclesiastical insiders were only adding to the confusion. Sounding similar to his Presbyterian contemporary J. Gresham Machen, Maier described "modern infidelity" as "more repulsive and damnable" because

> today the persecutors of our Savior are zealous in their appropriation of the Christian name and profuse in their exultation of the man Jesus; today opposition to Christ is disguised as the modern message of the Christian Church. . . . Mock loyalty to Christ is the traitorous spirit beneath the Judas kiss.[4]

He complained, "The devices of the weather-vane pulpit are as froth that is blown away with every change of the wind: and these chameleon-like preachers, who can change their color to match every shade of popular flavor, only lead men more deeply into sloughs of

---

[3]Walter A. Maier, *The Lutheran Hour: Winged Words to Modern America* (St. Louis: Concordia, 1931), 28, 163.
[4]Maier, *Lutheran Hour*, 108-9.

despair."[5] Interestingly, in a 1945 radio Christmas sermon, Maier approvingly quoted C. S. Lewis's insistence that one not accept Jesus "as a mighty teacher" but decide whether he "was, and is, the Son of God." The Lutheran concluded with the Oxford don's admonition: "Don't let us come with any patronizing nonsense about His being a great human teacher. He hasn't left that open to us. He didn't intend to."[6]

In striking alignment, Fulton Sheen described how "modern religion is feeding souls husks," indifferent to the "supreme truth" offered by the true church, "namely that man is a fallen creature in need of the saving grace of Divine Redemption."[7] He complained about what he saw as the "curse of broadmindedness." "America, it is commonly said, is suffering from intolerance," observed Sheen:

> I believe it is truer to say that America is not suffering so much from intolerance as it is suffering from a false kind of tolerance: the tolerance of right and wrong, truth and error, virtue and vice, Christ and chaos! The man, in our country, who can make up his mind and hold certain truths with all the fervor of his soul, is called narrow-minded, whereas the man who cannot make up his mind is called broad-minded.[8]

On another occasion, the Monsignor noted, "Why, many a modern religious leader would regard you as a scoundrel if you told him that he was not a gentleman, but would only smile on you benignantly if you told him he was not a Christian."[9]

On his radio broadcasts, Sheen scolded haughty modernists, both inside and outside the church, for lacking a genuine commitment to finding truth, notwithstanding their supposed pursuit of knowledge. By

[5]Walter A. Maier, *Christ for Every Crisis: The Radio Messages Broadcast on the Second Lutheran Hour* (St. Louis: Concordia, 1935), 66-67.
[6]Walter A. Maier, *Let Us Return unto the Lord* (St. Louis: Concordia, 1947), 209.
[7]Fulton J. Sheen, *The Eternal Galilean* (Garden City, NY: Garden City Books, 1950), 188-89.
[8]Fulton J. Sheen, *Manifestations of Christ* (Washington, DC: National Council of Catholic Men, 1932), 68.
[9]Sheen, *Eternal Galilean*, 189.

"freeing" their twentieth-century minds from historical dogmas, modernists had hoodwinked themselves and others into embracing a false "progress" by which they "confused a step forward with a step in the right direction." Such untethered minds were "more interested in the search for truth than in the truth itself. . . . They knocked not to have the door of truth opened, but to listen to the sound of their knuckles; they asked not to receive the purposes of life, but to hear the tones of their own voices." He continued, "They loved to talk about the glorious quest for truth, but they were very careful to avoid discovering it."[10] Drawing on the same biblical character as had Maier, Sheen concluded, "Like Pilate of old, they asked for truth, then turned their backs on it lest they hear the answer." Put succinctly, "Modern prophets . . . would rather be up-to-date than right, rather be wrong than behind the times."[11]

To counter these mischievous, "up-to-date prophets," Sheen and Maier presented substantive, doctrinally rich homilies. They assured their listeners of the existence and apprehensibility of eternal truths, describing them in vivid terms. They spoke of scriptural authority trumping human judgments. They spoke of the crucifixion of Christ, emphasizing the very non-Docetic nature of his sufferings, and the reality of the resurrection. They expounded on the sufficiency of the atonement in detailed, orthodox, personal terms. They conveyed the gravity of sin, often cataloging offenses to God so that no one could claim an exemption. They laid out the personal "wages" of such sin in temporal and eternal terms and warned of their costs to the nation. In jeremiads, Sheen and Maier boldly attributed the devastation of the Depression and later the brutal world war, at least in part, to the sinfulness of the American people. They occasionally went so far as to call for national "days of humiliation," not unlike the nation's Puritan forefathers. Notwithstanding such law-oriented rhetoric, however, it should be understood that what made these clerics

---

[10]Fulton J. Sheen, *Freedom and Peace* (Huntington, IN: Our Sunday Visitor, 1941), 11-13.
[11]Sheen, *Eternal Galilean*, 104.

effective was the equal fervor with which they proclaimed the *gospel*, assuring their ethereal congregants of the abundant grace that awaited the penitent sinner.

Maier and Sheen then encouraged their listeners to animate their faith commitments in specific ways. They extolled the virtues of sanctified living as a divinely adopted being, of godly marriages and foundational family structures, of devout prayer habits and devotional reading, of self-sacrifice and service to others, of humility in one's endeavors and judgments, and of witnessing to one's faith in the workplace, classroom, and community. Without wandering into political commentary, Maier and Sheen added to their proclamatory relevance by connecting biblical truths to the times in which they lived. Not unlike C. S. Lewis, both men had achieved considerable erudition and had careers within the academy, yet they frequently cautioned against the hubris they saw among the learned who scoffed at revealed truths. They called out progressive preachers who presumed to instruct on matters of public policy but failed to speak of sin and redemption and Christ's divinity. While commending scientific inquiry and the pursuit of knowledge, they both railed against scientists and other scholars who reduced humans to cosmic accidents and dismissed the role of the Creator. They were particularly wary of so-called experts within certain fields (e.g., psychology, sociology) whom they viewed as rationalizing away the sinful condition of individuals. To be clear, they generally affirmed the validity of such areas of study but indicted those practitioners whose conclusions dismissed the role of personal responsibility and repentance.

While their preaching contained substantial, often rarefied, theology, they avoided doctrinal assertions that were specific to their respective denominations. Though their radio programs bore the names of their ecclesiastical affiliations, both men went out of their way to avoid theological tedium and appeal to listeners across the denominational spectrum and beyond. Their preaching, however, represented anything but least-common-denominator religiosity or Christianity. Rather, it exposited core doctrines that demonstrated God's perfect moral standards, the listeners' manifest inability to meet these standards, and the only avenue by which such fallen humans could be reconciled to this holy God. In short, they presented what might be characterized as "mere Christianity."

Just as the American reception of C. S. Lewis's works is instructive, so is the response to Maier and Sheen on network radio. It should be understood that the previously mentioned size of their audiences put them in the same league as top entertainment programs of the day. Popular periodicals (e.g., *Time, Collier's, Newsweek, Saturday Evening Post, Look*) often profiled Sheen and Maier, noting that such "gospel spellbinders of the kilocycle lanes have bigger audiences than the Bob Hopes, Jack Bennys, and Charlie McCarthys."[12] But unlike their entertainer peers, these broadcasters offered something more substantive than diversionary laughs and serial drama. They played a role that went beyond their thirty-minute programs and was genuinely pastoral in nature. Just as C. S. Lewis sometimes felt overwhelmed by the volume of mail he received from readers, Maier's and Sheen's radio broadcasts generated tens of thousands of letters each week. Correspondents not only shared highly personal stories of how the broadcasts had affected their lives but often asked specific biblical and theological questions or requested pastoral guidance with a problem. Both preachers employed massive clerical staffs to help them to thoughtfully respond to their letter-writing "parishioners."

What are we to make of the American mainstream media's largely enthusiastic response to C. S. Lewis's multifaceted literary output in the 1930s and 1940s? The players within the media understood what

----

[12]Ben Gross, "The World's Largest Congregation," *Pageant* (February 1945): 119-23.

mainstream American culture wanted and to some degree shared those appetites. Whether looking for reinforcement of held Christian beliefs, or genuinely seeking foundational truths during turbulent times, or just stepping back to question intellectual trends that eagerly traded ancient truth claims for scientific explanations and human judgments, participants in the American experience wanted to be challenged. They were inclined to think for themselves but were eager to glean wisdom and knowledge from compelling sources in the process, and the "crystal clear well of thought" that Lewis offered was just such a source. So was the sturdy, topical theological oratory of Walter Maier and Fulton Sheen.[13] These were men of great learning, but they shared their learning and their convictions in inviting ways for their common readers and listeners. Within a text on medieval scholarship, Lewis referenced Mickey Mouse. In the middle of a sermon on Christian witness, Maier spoke of the St. Louis Browns in the World Series. Partway through a weighty sermon on the purpose of God's law, Sheen inserted a humorous analogy about filling one's automobile tank with Chanel No. 5. These men were erudite, but accessibly so.

In addition to wanting to be challenged in seeking truth, Americans were also open to being challenged in their personal conduct. Sheen once commented that humans "want something that makes demands on them, and possesses both their bodies and their souls."[14] As remarkable as it is, readers and listeners of these three Christian thinkers did not recoil from admonition for sinful behavior in a radio sermon, or warped intellectual priorities within a science-fiction tale, or examples of satanic influence that hit a bit close to home in the schemes of Uncle Screwtape.

---

[13]Interestingly, in his autobiography, Sheen credits Lewis, along with G. K. Chesterton, as being the greatest influences on his own writing. See Fulton J. Sheen, *Treasure in Clay: The Autobiography of Fulton J. Sheen* (New York: Society for the Propagation of the Faith, 1980), 83.
[14]Fulton J. Sheen, *Our Wounded World* (Washington, DC: National Council of Catholic Men, 1937), 41-42.

When C. S. Lewis appeared on the cover of *Time* magazine in 1947, the editors noted that he had a "talent for putting old-fashioned truths into a modern idiom . . . writing about religion for a generation of religion-hungry readers brought up on a diet of 'scientific' jargon and Freudian cliches."[15] Fulton Sheen and Walter Maier played similar roles. They may have been apostles to the skeptics, but they were also apostles to the receptive. Father James Maguire, as Noll quotes him in chapter one, more succinctly observes that Lewis just said "very many things that desperately need to be said." The culture into which Lewis, Maier, and Sheen spoke concluded the same of all three.

---

[15]"Don v. Devil," *Time*, September 8, 1974.

3

PROTESTANTS ALSO APPROVE

(BUT EVANGELICALS ONLY SLOWLY)

MARK A. NOLL

AS FOR THE READING PUBLIC IN GENERAL, so it was also for American Protestants: from the time that *The Screwtape Letters* appeared, C. S. Lewis received consistent and mostly positive attention. The historical record of Protestant responses, however, contains surprises, especially as recorded in a book sponsored by the Wade Center at Wheaton College. In recent decades the Center has been a leader among many other organizations, publications, colleges, clubs, reading circles, and church groups of evangelical persuasion in sustained fascination with all things related to the books and life of C. S. Lewis. The surprise is how late and how cautiously the evangelicals who would soon stand at the head of the line among Lewis's admirers responded to his works. The other surprise is where the most enthusiastic Protestant response came from. Representatives of the main denominations, which evangelicals and fundamentalists thought were being lost to theological modernism, with one exception greeted Lewis's books almost as enthusiastically as did American Catholics. Again, as with Catholic and mainstream reactions, these responses tell us a great deal about the

Protestant communities where Lewis was read during the war years and immediately thereafter.

The primary focus of this chapter is Lewis's reception by mainline Protestants and then by those who were in the process of rebranding themselves not as fundamentalists but now as evangelicals. At the end, however, we also pause to reflect on how the reception of Lewis in that distant era may instruct those of us today who value what he wrote and how he wrote it.

MAINLINE PROTESTANTS

The outlier among the strongly positive response to Lewis among those who would later be known as mainline Protestants was the "undenominational" weekly, *The Christian Century*. Charles Morrison, its moving spirit as editor from 1908 to 1947, viewed his magazine as the flagship periodical for the socially pro- gressive, ecumenically minded, and intellectually up-to-date denominations: Episcopalians, Congregationalists, northern Presbyterians, United Methodists, Lutherans not in the Missouri or Wisconsin Synods, northern Baptists, and Disciples of Christ. In the words of Elesha Coffman, under Morrison the *Century* led in "building a case for [these Protestants'] status as shepherds of the national soul."[1]

In the four years after the American publication of *The Screwtape Letters*, the *Century* reviewed or provided brief notices of six different books as well as a profile of Lewis by an Episcopal priest written after he had visited Lewis in Oxford. Along with some commendation and the by-now routine recognition of Lewis's "brilliant style," *The Christian Century*'s overall tone was patronizing: "his whimsicality was rather forced"; "his confident though rather naïve faith"; it would

---

[1]Elesha J. Coffman, *The Christian Century and the Rise of the Protestant Mainline* (New York: Oxford University Press, 2013), 3.

be better if Lewis "had a higher opinion of man"; Lewis as a writer was "too much at ease in Zion."[2]

The most interesting part of the *Century* profile written by the Episcopal priest, George Anderson, was not a literary judgment but fresh information about Lewis and W. H. Auden. It turned out that Auden was "a devout communicant" of Anderson's parish in Swarthmore, Pennsylvania, and that Auden had "enthusiastically introduced" his rector to Lewis's *Screwtape Letters*. (Chapter two details Auden's favorable review of *The Great Divorce*.) According to Anderson, when Lewis heard that Auden had recommended *Screwtape*, Lewis was taken by "the fact that the poet's recent works reflect a strong interest in religion, especially from the viewpoint of orthodox Christian theology." Yet Anderson himself seemed mostly bemused that Lewis was baffled by the works of Søren Kierkegaard, had difficulty following the reasoning of Reinhold Niebuhr, had not "read much" of Karl Barth, and "confessed ignorance of existentialism."[3] The visiting Episcopal rector, unlike Auden, his parishioner, seemed more interested in what Lewis had not read than what he had written.

By contrast, every other corner of the Protestant mainline that noted Lewis in these years expressed considerable satisfaction about what Lewis had in fact written. A harbinger of this approval came from Canada in a series of reviews published in *The Queen's Quarterly* from Queen's University, Kingston, Ontario. Nathaniel Miklem, an

---

[2]Note on *The Screwtape Letters*, *Christian Century*, March 24, 1943, 363; note on *The Case for Christianity*, *Christian Century*, September 29, 1943, 1105 ("whimsicality"); Talmage C. Johnson, review of *The Problem of Pain*, *Christian Century*, December 1, 1943, 1400 ("opinion of man"); note on *Christian Behaviour*, *Christian Century*, January 26, 1944, 114 ("naïve faith"); note on *Beyond Personality*, *Christian Century*, March 29, 1944, 410; Gaius Glenn Atkins, review of *Miracles*, *Christian Century*, December 3, 1947, 1486-87 ("brilliant style," "at ease in Zion").
[3]George C. Anderson, "C. S. Lewis: Foe of Humanism," *Christian Century*, December 25, 1946, 1562-63. On Lewis's earlier, mixed opinions about Auden's poetry, see several comments in *Books, Broadcasts, and the War, 1931–1949*, vol. 2 of *The Collected Letters of C. S. Lewis*, ed. Walter Hooper (San Francisco: HarperSanFrancisco, 2004): C. S. Lewis to Leo Baker, June 24, 1936, 197 (favorable); C. S. Lewis to Warren Lewis, July 20, 1940, 424 (unfavorable); C. S. Lewis to J. M. Thompson, July 25, 1940, 429 (unfavorable); Lewis to E. R. Eddison, November 16, 1942, 536 (unfavorable).

English Baptist who had opposed Britain's participation in the First World War, taught New Testament at Queen's from 1927 to 1932.[4] After Miklem returned to England as the head of Oxford University's Mansfield College, he continued to write for *The Queen's Quarterly*. His regular reports on new British books meant that his review of *The Screwtape Letters* was its first notice in North America ("those who like the taste of this hell-brew must buy this book"). Later, also in advance of other North American reviews, Miklem published positive assessments of *A Preface to Paradise Lost* ("This book, apart from its merits as a piece of literary criticism, has its value as a piece of religious interpretation") and *The Abolition of Man* ("Mr. Lewis shows by brilliant illustration and in excellent literary form how the Nihilism which flowers in the 'ideology' . . . of the Nazi Party finds expression . . . among ourselves, even in the most respectable of school text-books").[5]

When representatives of the United States' mainline Protestants followed with their reviews, they echoed Miklem's praise much more than the pooh-poohing of *The Christian Century*. One of the most interesting indications of that approval came in the summer of 1943, when the periodical *Religion in Life* published an article it had solicited from Lewis himself. This article, titled "The Poison of Subjectivism," précised the argument against ethical relativism that Lewis had just published in England as *The Abolition of Man* but that would not appear in North America until several years later. *Religion in Life* was a quarterly sponsored by the publishing house of the United Methodist Church. The next year, 1944, the same periodical

---

[4]The Theological College at Queen's served the United Church of Canada, which, in 1925, had brought together Methodists, Congregationalists, and a majority of Canada's Presbyterians.

[5]Nathaniel Miklem, review of *The Screwtape Letters*, *Queen's Quarterly* 49 (1942): 285-86; Miklem, review of *A Preface to Paradise Lost*, *Queen's Quarterly* 50 (1943): 103; Miklem, review of *The Abolition of Man*, *Queen's Quarterly* 51 (1944): 333. On Miklem, see Marguerite Van Die, ed., *From Heaven Down to Earth: A Century of Chancellor's Lectures at Queen's Theological College* (Kingston, Ontario: Queen's Theological College, 1992), 51.

ran a highly favorable review by a Lutheran pastor from New York City, Paul Scherer, of a reissue of *The Pilgrim's Regress* and of Lewis's recently published broadcast talk, *Christian Behaviour*. What Scherer thought of Lewis's work could not be mistaken when he said concerning the latter, "There is something clever and jaunty about it from beginning to end, as there is about all of his work; yet something tremendously in earnest: apt and homely and forceful, full of asides, yet deep and sure and persuasive."[6] This Lutheran writing for a Methodist-sponsored publication had only a positive opinion.

The same was true across the board. American Episcopalians expressed their hearty approval of the same broadcast talks that the Lutheran Scherer had praised ("brief, sound, thought-provoking essays"), as well in long and short reviews of *The Problem of Pain*.[7] *Theology Today*, published by the Presbyterian Princeton Theological Seminary, was at the time the widest-circulating theological quarterly in the world. A substantial article in its pages from 1945 offered a positive account of every Lewis book published to date, except for the literary studies. It began by reporting, "The two most popular theologians in the English-speaking world today are Dorothy Sayers and C. S. Lewis . . . because 'they have made the language of Christianity live afresh for their fellow countrymen.'" The article also paused in a lengthy footnote to put down the putdown of Lewis that had been published by Alister Cooke the previous year: "Where he intends to be scathing he is only petulant, where serious, only irrelevant." Two years later in the same journal, Princeton Seminary's leading theologian, Hugh Kerr, published a short appreciation of

---

[6]C. S. Lewis, "The Poison of Subjectivism," *Religion in Life* 12 (Summer 1943): 356-65; Paul E. Scherer, review of *The Pilgrim's Regress* and *Christian Behaviour*, *Religion in Life* 13 (Autumn 1944): 615-16.

[7]W. F. W., review of *Christian Behaviour*, *Anglican Theological Review* 26 (July 1944): 191-92; Charles L. Street, review of *The Problem of Pain*, *Anglican Theological Review* 26 (July 1944): 185; Ashley Simpson, "C. S. Lewis—A Crusading Intellect," *The Southern Churchman*, December 14, 1946, 5-6 (mostly a review of *The Problem of Pain*).

Lewis's anthology of George MacDonald's writings; it concluded with the opinion that many readers "will feel that C. S. Lewis is much more interesting" than MacDonald.[8] *Interpretation*, the theological quarterly of the Presbyterians' Union Seminary in Richmond, Virginia, joined the northern Presbyterians when it ran a favorable review of Lewis's "brilliantly presented" *Abolition of Man*.[9]

This same book also received high marks from another theological quarterly, *Review and Expositor*.[10] This journal came from the Southern Baptist seminary in Louisville, Kentucky, that was widely regarded as that denomination's leading theological institution. It was at a time, moreover, when leaders of the Louisville seminary viewed themselves as closer to the main Protestant denominations than to fundamentalists or the new evangelical networks that were just being formed.

A final indication of approval from these quarters (and quarterlies) appeared in several positive notices in *The Journal of Bible and Religion*, which was published by the interdenominational—but almost exclusively Protestant—National Association of Bible Instructors. This journal was later renamed *The Journal of the American Academy of Religion* to reflect the evolution of the association away from strictly Protestant concerns to the much wider interests of the American Academy of Religion (another later name change). In the 1940s, however, *The Journal of Bible and Religion* still functioned as a largely Protestant periodical serving Bible professors who taught in a wide range of colleges and universities.

Its first review of Lewis appeared in 1944, with a positive notice for *The Problem of Pain* written by a professor from Swarthmore College, who praised Lewis as "one of the ablest and most persuasive

---

[8]Edward D. Myers, "The Religious Works of C. S. Lewis," *Theology Today* 1 (January 1945): 545-48 (footnote on Cooke, 545); Hugh Thompson Kerr Jr., "C. S. Lewis Pays a Debt," *Theology Today* 4 (July 1947): 259-60.

[9]Andrew K. Rule, review of *The Abolition of Man*, *Interpretation* 1 (July 1947): 408-9.

[10]W. O. Carver, review of *The Abolition of Man*, *Review and Expositor* 44 (July 1947): 375-77.

proponents of positive Christianity to be found among literary figures of the present time." Two years later the August 1946 issue of the journal included a Lewis trifecta. In one article a scholarly reviewer praised *That Hideous Strength* as "an absorbing story." The Beloit professor whom we have seen writing about Lewis for the secular press supplied the other two articles. It was Chad Walsh with a positive review of Lewis's introduction to a modern edition of fourth-century bishop-theologian Athanasius's *On the Incarnation of the Word* and with a lengthy article comparing Lewis's Ransom Trilogy to the imaginative works of Aldous Huxley. Walsh commended the bleak view of Huxley's well-known fantasy, *Brave New World*, as well as Huxley's advocacy of *The Perennial Philosophy* as an alternative to modern secularism. But he obviously thought Lewis's novels responded more persuasively to deeper human needs: "He drives home his message in a more subtle way: by creating a picture of life on the different planets which makes no sense unless Christianity is true, and by making the picture so sensuously real that it is difficult to put down one of his novels and dismiss it as 'mere escape fiction.'"[11]

The verdict on Lewis from these several representatives of the United States' informal Protestant establishment was remarkably consistent: He writes brilliantly. He argues persuasively. He inspires the imagination. He presents orthodox Christianity believably. If *The Christian Century*'s response to Lewis anticipated later fragmentation and liberalization among American mainline Protestants, into the late 1940s that mainline contained a substantial center, not only willing but eager to applaud what, in a term from Charles Taylor, could be called C. S. Lewis's vigorous Christian "imaginary."[12]

---

[11]John M. Moore, review of *The Problem of Pain, Journal of Bible and Religion* 12 (May 1944): 123-24; Carl E. Purinton, review of *That Hideous Strength, Journal of Bible and Religion* 14 (August 1946): 186-87; Chad Walsh, review of *The Incarnation of the Word of God, Journal of Bible and Religion* 14 (August 1946): 176; Walsh, "Aldous Huxley and C. S. Lewis: Novelists of Two Religions," *Journal of Bible and Religion* 14 (August 1946): 139-43.

[12]Charles Taylor, *Modern Social Imaginaries* (Durham, NC: Duke University Press, 2003).

EVANGELICALS HESITANT OR AMBIGUOUS

The story for American evangelicals was more complicated—
including some lightweight approval, some serious theological dis-
quiet, some nervousness, but also some hints of enthusiastic
appreciation. It began with *The Christian Herald*, which had been a
major publication since the late nineteenth century. A New York
City minister, Thomas De Witt Talmage, and an energetic entre-
preneur, Louis Klopsch, put the magazine on the map by emphasizing
missionary outreach abroad, ministry to the down-and-out in New
York City, and programs of international aid that surpassed even the
work of the Red Cross.[13] Daniel Poling, an ordained United Brethren
minister strongly committed to prohibition, personal holiness, the
separation of church and state, and the youth program Christian
Endeavor, revitalized the magazine when he took over as editor in 1927.

Poling's Wesleyan-leaning monthly was the one evangelical publication to acknowledge Lewis's works early and often. It offered two- or
three-sentence commendations of *The Screwtape Letters, Out of the
Silent Planet, The Case for Christianity,* and *That Hideous Strength*—
in fact, two short notices for this third volume of the Ransom Trilogy.
For *The Great Divorce* the commendation ("compressed, dynamic, delightful reading") extended to two short paragraphs.[14] Still, the greatest
amount of text in *The Christian Herald* on Lewis came from advertisements that Macmillan placed in the magazine.[15]

The *Herald's* two short notices of *That Hideous Strength* spoke
tellingly of the nation's general evangelical readership. The first

[13]See Heather Curtis, *Holy Humanitarians: American Evangelicals and Global Aid* (Cambridge, MA: Harvard University Press, 2018).
[14]Review of *The Screwtape Letters, The Christian Herald* (April 1943): 48; review of *Out of the Silent Planet, The Christian Herald* (December 1943): 66, 68; review of *The Case for Christianity, The Christian Herald* (December 1943): 70; review of *That Hideous Strength, The Christian Herald* (July 1946): 56; review of *That Hideous Strength, The Christian Herald* (September 1946): 68; review of *The Great Divorce, The Christian Herald* (May 1946): 56-57.
[15]Macmillan advertisements, March 1946, 48, and May 1946, inside front cover (full page).

called the novel "another of its author's strange masterpieces" and said "its humor and satire are profound." But then the reviewer concluded by confessing that the book was "beyond my depth." Two months later the second review replaced this ambiguous judgment by concluding that the novel "leaves you always one small window of hope—and faith is at last the answer."[16]

In contrast to the positive but superficial treatments in *The Christian Herald*, lengthy, intelligent, but distinctly mixed responses came from the only other corner of the evangelical world that paid extended attention to Lewis in those years. That corner was occupied by the conservative Presbyterians who followed J. Gresham Machen as that learned New Testament scholar mounted an increasingly sharp critique of liberal trends in his denomination, the main body of northern Presbyterians. In 1929, these conservatives had established Westminster Theological Seminary in Philadelphia as a protest against mediating steps taken by Princeton Theological Seminary. In 1936, after Machen lost his ministerial credentials for founding an independent society to compete with the northern church's missionary agency, the conservatives broke away again, this time to set up a new denomination, the Orthodox Presbyterian Church.

Like the great majority of Lewis's American readers, the conservative Presbyterians appreciated the verve of his prose. Like some Catholics, they brought considerable learning to their reviews. But unlike all but a few Catholic reviewers, they focused their attention on the theological particulars of Lewis's articulation of the Christian faith. Beginning in 1944, ministers associated with Westminster Seminary published some of the era's most serious responses to Lewis's books. Almost a decade earlier, however, the most interesting American review of *The Pilgrim's Regress* had already been penned by one of Machen's acolytes writing in the monthly magazine of the new denomination.

---

[16]Review of *That Hideous Strength*, *The Christian Herald* (July 1946): 56; review of *That Hideous Strength*, *The Christian Herald* (September 1946): 68.

THE PRESBYTERIAN GUARDIAN   **117**

place where the next General Assembly will convene. The time: November 12-15, 1936. An important action governing the constituency and powers of that assembly follows:

The following persons shall be accounted accredited commissioners to that General Assembly:

1. Every minister in the Presbyterian Church of America.
2. One elder from every particular church in that communion, such particular churches to be formed in a manner to be prescribed by this Assembly.

That General Assembly shall have power to adopt the Constitution of the Presbyterian Church of America.

Striking reactions to the first General Assembly: Many remarked that this Assembly was the first really *deliberative* assembly in which they had ever participated. All were greatly impressed with the unfailing courtesy, patience and impartiality of the Moderator.

Roll of the Assembly

Ministers

Dean W. Adair, Philadelphia.
Samuel J. Allen, Carson, N. D.
Philip duB. Arcularius, Duryea, Pa.
Robert L. Atwell, Harrisville, Pa.
J. Oliver Buswell, Jr., Wheaton, Ill.
John P. Clelland, Wilmington, Del.
Peter De Ruiter, Nottingham, Pa.
Everett C. DeVelde, New Park, Pa.
Franklin S. Dyrness, Quarryville, Pa.
David Freeman, Philadelphia.

J. Enoch Faw, Westfield, N. J.
William H. MacCorkell, Philadelphia.
John B. Wright, Philadelphia.
Edwin W. Abbot, Luzerne, Pa.
W. T. Benedict, Forestville, Pa.
Gordon H. Clark, Philadelphia.
C. W. Clelland, Grove City, Pa.
James R. Cummings, Baltimore, Md.
R. C. Duffy, Branchton, Pa.
John Welsh Dulles, Philadelphia.
Thomas R. Galbraith, Wyncote, Pa.
Frank Blainer, Columbus, N. J.
Harold W. Hillegas, Merrill, Wis.
Allen R. Hood, Philadelphia.
W. E. McBride, Harrisville, Pa.
J. Herbert Rue, Merchantville, N. J.
W. R. Sibley, Seattle, Wash.
Bert W. Tennant, West Pittston, Pa.
Andrew H. Wakefield, Philadelphia.
John S. Wurts, Philadelphia.

In addition to the roll of voting members of the Assembly, the following persons who signified their inten-

tion of joining the Presbyterian Church of America were enrolled as associate members, and were given the privileges of the floor:

Rev. Charles Dana Chrisman, R. D. 1, New City, N. Y.
Rev. Leslie A. Dunn, Columbus, N. J.
Rev. Lewis J. Grotenhuis, Phillipsburg, N. J.
Rev. Robert S. Marsden, Middletown, Pa.
Rev. John C. Rankin, Worcester, N. Y.
Rev. Cornelius Van Til, Philadelphia, Pa.
Rev. Robert L. Vining, Mifflinburg, Pa.
Rev. Peter F. Wall, Chester, N. Y.
Rev. Walter V. Watson, Syracuse, N. Y.
Ruling Elder George B. Crippen, Worcester, N. Y.
Ruling Elder Samuel Scott, Williamstown, N. J.

A Modern Allegory
Reviewed by the Rev. HENRY G. WELBON

THE PILGRIM'S REGRESS, by C. S. Lewis, Sheed & Ward, Inc., New York. Printed in England, 1935.

IN SPITE of the title this is a modern pilgrim's progress. The author calls it, "An allegorical apology for Christianity.

The story begins with a boy who lived his youth in Puritania. He is taken to the Steward (the priest) who gives him a card of rules and tells him about the Landlord and the Black Hole. As the boy grows he is dissatisfied with these teachings and yields to sensual pleasure. The author leads his character from there through Roman-

Figure 3.1. The first serious attention to C. S. Lewis in an American Christian publication came from this article in *The Presbyterian Guardian* from June 1936.

That book's appearance from the Catholic publisher Sheed & Ward, its allegorical depiction of "Mother Kirk," and the praise it had garnered from Catholic reviewers created a misunderstanding of particular interest for Wheaton College. The review appeared in the June 22, 1936, issue of *The Presbyterian Guardian*. Its author was Henry Welbon, a Pennsylvania minister who would himself experience a church lockout, legal tussles, and much local controversy when he tried to take his congregation into the new church body.[17] The review was printed next to a list of commissioners to the first general assembly of the new denomination, a roll that included Wheaton's president, J. Oliver Buswell Jr.; the college's best-known professor, philosopher Gordon Clark; and several others with Wheaton connections.

Welbon's review of Lewis's biographical allegory was particularly striking for the way it combined startled appreciation with

---

[17]The lockout occurred shortly after the review appeared.

predictable reservations. Early in the review Welbon identified
Lewis as "an Englishman who is a Roman Catholic," but he nonetheless praised the book for exposing "the fallacies of various philosophies throughout the world today" with "lucid arguments in
simple direct sentences." At a time when most American Protestants
still regarded Catholicism with abhorrence, this one small group
of conservative Presbyterians was a partial exception, in large
part because of what J. Gresham Machen had written in a much-
publicized book from 1923, *Christianity and Liberalism*. That work
indicted all forms of Protestant modernism as anti-Christian, but
along the way Machen paused for the unconventional opinion that
confessional Protestants shared much more with traditional
Catholics than they did with liberal Protestants.[18] That argument
was opening enough for Welbon not to write off Lewis, even though,
as Welbon thought, he was a Catholic. Moreover, Welbon obviously
also appreciated the wide-ranging learning that informed *The
Pilgrim's Regress*. Thus, he concluded his review by writing,
"Although we do not agree with the author's theology, nevertheless
there is much that we have in common with the message of his
book. We greatly appreciated this unusual style of exposing the
fallacies of unbelief."[19]

An intriguing sequel followed. Apparently Welbon sent his review
to Lewis with a request for more information about the author.
Lewis's reply of September 18, 1936, immediately set Welbon straight
on the facts: Lewis was "born in Belfast" (he was not English) and was
"an Anglican Layman" (he was not a Roman Catholic). But Lewis also
took responsibility for "the mistake which led you, and has led others,
to make me a Papist" due to his allegorical depiction of "Mother Kirk."
With friends, Lewis was blunter in blaming Sheed & Ward for this

---

[18]J. Gresham Machen, *Christianity and Liberalism* (New York: Macmillan, 1923), 52.
[19]Henry G. Welbon, review of *The Pilgrim's Regress*, *Presbyterian Guardian*, June 22, 1936,
117, 141.

mix-up.[20] But to the American Welbon he set out in 1936 what would eventually become the gist of "mere Christianity." After telling how his own journey to faith had been assisted by an Anthroposophist (Owen Barfield, whom he does not name), the Presbyterian George MacDonald, the Catholic Dante, and another unnamed Catholic (J. R. R. Tolkien), Lewis then explained to Welbon why he was "at home" with this ecclesiastical mishmash: "they are all alike 'evangelical' in the Pauline sense, all concerned with the 'new creature,' and also because they are all genuine *supernaturalists*."[21] For our purposes, the most interesting thing about the Welbon review was that it represented the sole early notice of Lewis from the broadly evangelical part of the American religious landscape. After 1936, it was seven more years before that constituency produced anything more on Lewis.

When the conservative Westminster Presbyterians published their substantial reviews of Lewis's later books, Lewis's explanation to Welbon about why he favored the "mere Christianity" approach became a bone of contention. Although the five authors responsible for these reviews concentrated solely on Lewis's apologetical works, they resembled the more serious Catholic reviewers in the depth of their theological learning. The most appreciative of the five appeared in May 1944, when Paul Woolley, who served Westminster Seminary as professor of church history and also its registrar, published a long

---

[20]See C. S. Lewis to Arthur Greeves, December 7, 1935, in Hooper, *Collected Letters* 2:170: "My other bit of literary news is that Sheed and Ward have bought the *Regress* from Dent. I didn't much like having a book of mine, and specially a religious book, brought out by a Papist publisher: but as they seemed to think they could sell it, and Dents clearly couldn't, I gave in. I have been well punished: for Sheed, without any authority from me, has put a blurb on the inside of the jacket which says 'This story begins in Puritania (Mr. Lewis was brought up in Ulster)'—thus implying that the book is an attack on my own country and my own religion. If you ever come across any one who might be interested, explain as loudly as you can that I was not consulted & that the blurb is a damnable lie told to try and make Dublin riff-raff buy the book."
[21]C. S. Lewis to Henry Welbon, September 18, 1936 (C. S. Lewis Letter Collection, Marion E. Wade Center, Wheaton College, Wheaton, IL).

review of *The Problem of Pain* and the first two of Lewis's broadcast talks, *The Case for Christianity* and *Christian Behavior*.[22]

The Woolley essay review was unusual because it commended Lewis as highly as any American of the period while at the same time intimating the kind of criticism that other conservative Presbyterians would elaborate. Woolley's approval marked his very first sentences: "C. S. Lewis is one of the finest reasons for giving thanks to God which this reviewer has met for some time. He can be both a great source of knowledge and inspiration to Christians and, at the same time, one of the most powerful apologetes for Christianity to this generation."[23] He then went on to praise Lewis's writing as "full of verve and most appropriate to the needs of the day" and to commend the first two space novels, which he was not reviewing, as "fascinating . . . because they base fantasy upon Christian theology."

According to Woolley, *The Problem of Pain* showed how "God uses pain as an instrument to accomplishing his purpose of teaching man fundamental lessons that every one is forced to learn if he is to adjust himself with any success to the created universe as it exists." Lewis's *Case for Christianity* was "a brilliant statement in non-theological language of some elementary, but fundamental, reasons for being a Christian." Woolley claimed that Lewis's booklet *Christian Behaviour* was convincing on "the meaning of marriage" and in pointing out that "pride is just about the hardest thing on earth to detect in one's self." The same book also taught a lesson desperately needed by "American fundamentalis[ts]," who needed to realize that things such as beer or the cinema were not dangerous in themselves but in how they were used. Woolley paused to observe that if fundamentalists

---

[22] As a personal aside, I was privileged to enjoy brief contact with Professor Woolley in his later years at Westminster; he seemed to me a true Christian gentleman of genuine humility, generosity, and historical wisdom.

[23] All quotations in this and following paragraphs are from Paul Woolley, essay review of *The Problem of Pain, The Case for Christianity*, and *Christian Behaviour, Westminster Theological Journal* 6 (May 1944): 210-14.

"could learn this fact, I dare say it would be one of the biggest moves toward starting a revival that that movement could take." Then he closed the essay with another enthusiastic outburst: "These volumes are the 'find' of the year for any literate Christian."

Yet in Woolley's cornucopia of praise came also some theological concerns.

A minor matter was that, although he thought Lewis's treatment of marriage in *Christian Behaviour* was superb, he considered what Lewis wrote on sex itself confused and unhelpful. More important to Woolley was Lewis's treatment of innate human capacities for understanding moral or religious truths. He approved Lewis's argument that if a person did not believe in objective morality, that person could not trust their own reason either to argue against moral objectivity or to deny the existence of God. Yet when Woolley paraphrased Lewis's point, he recast it to fit into the approach to apologetics for which Westminster was renowned: "In other words, thinking and rational argument that do not begin with God as a premise are useless and prove nothing." The shift in starting point from belief in objective morality to belief in God was the crucial matter.

To Woolley several mistakes reinforced one another. In *The Problem of Pain*, he thought Lewis erred in viewing sin in terms of individual actions and not recognizing the fundamental importance of "total depravity." Woolley also did not "believe that anthropological investigation indicated that the agreement between men of different backgrounds about the 'Law of Rules about Right and Wrong' is as thoroughgoing and uniform as Lewis thinks." As a consequence, because Lewis did not insist that all true reasoning must begin with explicit belief in God, his account of the atonement suffered.

In terms other Westminster theologians would use, Lewis did not take seriously enough "the noetic effect of the fall." He did not realize that universal human agreement in objective morality was not the same as presupposing the God of Scripture as the beginning point of all true moral judgment. In addition, as illustrated by his account of the atonement, Lewis confused the categories of Creator and creation by talking about believers coming to share in the divine life rather than simply being born again and renewed by God's grace.

The criticisms that for Woolley merely seasoned a positive commendation loomed larger when other Orthodox Presbyterians turned to Lewis's books. Two reviews, which critiqued Lewis's *Beyond Personality*, echoed the complaints of some Jesuits that Lewis had ascribed too much divinity to persons of Christian faith. Cornelius Van Til, the chief architect of Westminster's presuppositional apologetics, contended that when Lewis wrote about the believer's divine sonship and then the Trinity, he meandered off into "a vague, pantheising form of Christianity." Because, according to Van Til, Lewis misunderstood "the creator-creature relationship . . . the main argument of the book is destructive of the evangelical faith."[24] A longer, slightly more charitable review in the *Westminster Theological Journal* praised Lewis for puncturing wishy-washy modernist views of Christianity. But critique soon followed: in his discussion of the Trinity and of the believer's new life in Christ, Lewis was faulted for "clothing some of the most precious mysteries of our holy faith in the grave clothes of perilous speculation" and for not showing "due deference to Scripture."[25]

Six months later another reviewer for the *Westminster Theological Journal* praised Lewis's *The Great Divorce* as "an unorthodox defense of orthodoxy." In addition, he called it a book for "all adult readers" and "especially helpful to clergymen." Yet *The Great Divorce* also fell short because the book was "very man-centered." Lewis, in the reviewer's eye, treated sin as simply self-defeating, without a proper acknowledgment of "God's righteous wrath and sentence."[26]

---

[24]Cornelius Van Til, review of *Beyond Personality*, *United Evangelical Action*, May 15, 1946, 15.
[25]Jacob Dirk Eppinga, review of *Beyond Personality*, *Westminster Theological Journal* 8 (May 1946): 225-27.
[26]A. Culver Gordon, review of *The Great Divorce*, *Westminster Theological Journal* 9 (November 1946): 110-11.

The same ambivalence characterized a review of *The Abolition of Man* in November 1947 by a young Orthodox Presbyterian minister, Edmund Clowney.[27] He opined that Christian believers should applaud Lewis's attack on modern educational theories that promoted ethical relativism and denied objective moral values. Yet in his view, what Lewis wrote is "somewhat disturbing, coming from one who identifies himself as a Christian." The problem lay in treating "a general natural law referred to as the Tao" as in any way equivalent with "the Scriptural concept of the truth of [God's] law." Clowney, in other words, thought Lewis erred in how he presented the natural law, which incidentally was the feature of Lewis's works that Catholic critics so much appreciated. To Clowney, "the principles of natural law" were as "twisted and deformed in ancient Paganism . . . as in modern relativism." For a proper Christian consideration of "ultimate moral principles," it was imperative to begin with the God who says, "I am the Lord thy God, who brought thee out of the land of Egypt." Only that specifically biblical starting point, and not merely the common human belief in moral absolutes, could produce true love to God and genuine benevolence to the neighbor.[28]

In sum, Edmund Clowney's critique faulted Lewis for a strategic theological error. Yes, his forthright Christianity and his creative imagination should be welcomed. But by reasoning from ordinary human experience to specific Christian belief, this conservative Presbyterian thought Lewis undermined scriptural Christianity by replacing the infallible God with self-centered human instincts.

---

[27]Clowney, Wheaton class of 1939 and later the president of Westminster Seminary, remained a good friend of the college, where he was a regular guest preacher in its chapel services. Sometime in the late 1980s or early 1990s I heard him offer a meditation on 2 Sam 23:16-17 that, in reflecting on David's pouring out of the water his troops had brought to him at peril of their lives, became the most powerful gospel sermon I have ever heard.

[28]Edmund Clowney, review of *The Abolition of Man*, *Westminster Theological Journal* 10 (November 1947): 79-81.

Orlin R. Kohli, Wheaton, Ill.

Figure 3.2. By the early 1950s, Professor Clyde S. Kilby of Wheaton College stood for a growing number of American evangelicals who were expressing great appreciation for C. S. Lewis's Christian point of view as well as for simply his creative literary ability.

An intriguing follow-up to this Westminster critique may have factored into the creation of what would become the Wade Center at Wheaton College. In 1955, Cornelius Van Til published a major statement of his theological position in a book titled *The Defense of the Faith*. In it he expanded his criticism to say that Lewis, like Thomas Aquinas, mistakenly treated humankind's basic problem as finitude rather than rebellion against God. According to Van Til, Lewis erred further by believing that the general human sense of objective morality was the same as what the repentant sinner found in following the God of the Bible. As a consequence, "the 'gospel according to St. Lewis' is too much a compromise with the ideas of the natural man to constitute a clear challenge in our day."[29]

By the time Van Til published this work, Wheaton College professor Clyde Kilby had become fascinated with Lewis's work; he also knew what Van Til, as well as Edmund Clowney, had written. With characteristic directness, Kilby wrote to Lewis in January 1959, asking him how he responded to Van Til's criticism of *Beyond Personality*. Lewis replied almost immediately, but curtly, to make two points. First, it was scriptural (John 1:12) to say that believers became "sons of God," a belief in keeping with Athanasius's statement that "God became Man that men might become gods." Second, Lewis by no means wrote, as the Westminster critics contended, that humans could make this ascent by their own efforts.[30] The exchange of letters certainly answered Kilby's question but may also have encouraged the idea that Wheaton would be a good place for a special collection of Lewis's letters as well as for his published works.

The criticism of the Westminster Presbyterians, who were the only evangelical Protestants in the 1940s to engage with Lewis at any depth, certainly deserves theological reflection in its own right. But that criticism, along with the Kilby-Lewis exchange from the late 1950s, which showed the Wheaton professor more sympathetic to

---

[29]Cornelius Van Til, *The Defense of the Faith* (Philadelphia: Presbyterian & Reformed, 1955), 75-77, here 77.

[30]C. S. Lewis to Clyde Kilby, January 20, 1959, in *The Collected Letters of C. S. Lewis*, ed. Walter Hooper (San Francisco: HarperSanFrancisco, 2004), 3:1013-14.

Lewis than to Van Til, raises a most interesting question. How and why did the evangelical landscape shift between the mid-1940s and the late 1950s? In fact, hints were already beginning to appear in answer to that question, and not only in *The Christian Herald*.

EVANGELICALS BEGIN TO APPRECIATE

To be sure, in the leading journals that acted as arbiters for the fundamentalist-evangelical world, the future was hard to see. In December 1943, *Moody Monthly* did praise Lewis as "a master of analogy" for his *Case for Christianity* and also commended Lewis for what he wrote about the instinctive human belief in "Right and Wrong" (the very argument that made the conservative Presbyterians nervous). Yet more than two-thirds of the *Monthly*'s short review offered reservations. It wondered how effective any apologetics could be in convincing nonbelievers and found "open to question" what Lewis wrote about the sacraments, the "Christ life" of the believer, the atonement, and the possibility that some who have not heard of Christ might be redeemed in Christ.[31]

Similarly, in 1946, *United Evangelical Action*, the magazine of the National Association of Evangelicals, included Lewis's *Beyond Personality* in a list of twenty-five books "not evangelical in sentiment yet significant for the evangelical mind." Probably following the criticism of Cornelius Van Til, its one-sentence comment described the book as a "stimulating but inadequate treatment of the Christian idea of God."[32]

In the same year, however, the *Sunday School Times* published two short notices that suggested a more positive view. This weekly was

---

[31]Review of *The Case for Christianity, Moody Monthly* (December 1943): 239.

[32]Note on *Beyond Personality, United Evangelical Action*, April 30, 1946, 15. A more positive review, though still with reservations, came when E. J. Carnell, a leading neo-evangelical scholar, provided a short note on *Miracles* for the same publication. He called the book "a real contribution to Christian apologetics" but nonetheless thought that Lewis gave "evidence of theological uncertainty at points," especially in treating miracles in the Old Testament and, in general, "the relation between miracles and the canon." *United Evangelical Action*, February 1, 1948, 24.

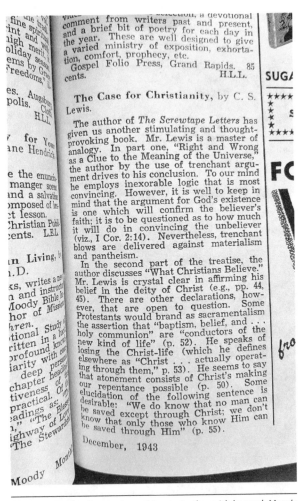

comment from writers past and present, and a brief bit of poetry for each day in the year. These are well designed to give a varied ministry of exposition, exhortation, comfort, prophecy, etc.

Gospel Folio Press, Grand Rapids. 85 cents.   H.L.L.

The Case for Christianity, by C. S. Lewis.

The author of *The Screwtape Letters* has given us another stimulating and thought-provoking book. Mr. Lewis is a master of analogy. In part one, "Right and Wrong as a Clue to the Meaning of the Universe," the author by the use of trenchant argument drives to his conclusion. To our mind he employs inexorable logic that is most convincing. However, it is well to keep in mind that the argument for God's existence is one which will confirm the believer's faith; it is to be questioned as to how much it will do in convincing the unbeliever (viz., I Cor. 2:14). Nevertheless, trenchant blows are delivered against materialism and pantheism.

In the second part of the treatise, the author discusses "What Christians Believe." Mr. Lewis is crystal clear in affirming his belief in the deity of Christ (e.g., pp. 44, 45). There are other declarations, however, that are open to question. Some Protestants would brand as sacramentalism the assertion that "baptism, belief, and . . . holy communion" are "conductors of the new kind of life" (p. 52). He speaks of losing the Christ-life (which he defines elsewhere as "Christ . . . actually operating through them," p. 53). He seems to say that atonement consists of Christ's making our repentance possible (p. 50). Some elucidation of the following sentence is desirable: "We do know that no man can be saved except through Christ; we don't know that only those who know Him can be saved through Him" (p. 55).

December, 1943

Moody Monthly

Figure 3.3. The first review of Lewis in the widely read *Moody Monthly* mingled admiration with a number of serious reservations.

edited by Philip Howard Jr. Its provision of aids for Sunday school teachers made it probably the magazine that circulated most widely among northern fundamentalists. In a 1946 review of *Beyond Personality*, the *Times* described Lewis as "one of those wise men who has yielded to the gospel and who seems to believe it with all his heart." While questioning Lewis in believing that "there are people in

Figure 3.4. Elisabeth Howard, the Wheaton College student who told her parents about C. S. Lewis, would soon write (as Elisabeth Elliot) with increasing sensitivity about the problems as well as the triumphs of missionary service.

other religions who belong to Christ without knowing it," this short review ended by calling the book "most stimulating."[33] Earlier in the year, a paragraph in the same magazine reported as a news item that Lewis, "an Oxford don" who had been "delivered from agnosticism, is now giving his testimony in book and broadcast to the saving

---

[33]Review of *Beyond Personality*, *Sunday School Times*, November 5, 1946, 914-15.

Christ." The same notice added a few sentences that Lewis wrote, though without indicating the source.[34]

It is just possible that a personal connection lay behind the *Sunday School Times*'s new attention to C. S. Lewis. In early 1946, a Wheaton College sophomore informed her mother that she was greatly enjoying *The Screwtape Letters*. She wrote that the book was "clever, and really gives one an idea of Satan's subtle trickery. . . . I got a real blessing from it." Later that year the same student expanded her praise: "At present I am reading C. S. Lewis: *Perelandra*, a novel discussing life on Venus! It is tremendous. You all should read some of his works—especially *Screwtape Letters* if you haven't already."[35] The college student was Elisabeth Howard, who would marry Jim Elliot after they both graduated from Wheaton and then later write a moving book about the murder of her husband and four other missionaries in the Ecuadorian jungle.[36]

Elisabeth Howard's letters to the family responsible for editing the *Sunday School Times* anticipated the tidal wave of evangelical approval that lay only a few years into the future. Yet even as she was telling her parents about *Screwtape* and *Perelandra*, another venue had already begun to explain why evangelicals should pay attention. It was *HIS* magazine, the monthly publication serving InterVarsity Christian Fellowship. In February 1944, *HIS* ran a substantial extract from *The Case for Christianity*, where Lewis used the universal human sense of right and wrong to begin his account of the faith. (It was this same account that seemed merely humanistic to the Westminster Presbyterians.) A year and a half later, *HIS* offered a book review of *The Problem of Pain* that commended Lewis for saying that "if God is Love, He is something more than mere kindness." Then in a few more

---

[34]Untitled, *Sunday School Times*, February 9, 1946, 110.
[35]Elisabeth Howard to Katherine Howard, February 17, 1946, and November 11, 1946 (box 3, folder 5, Collection 278: Papers of Elisabeth Elliot, Wheaton College Billy Graham Center Archives, Wheaton College, Wheaton, IL).
[36]Elisabeth Elliot, *Through Gates of Splendor* (New York: Harper, 1958).

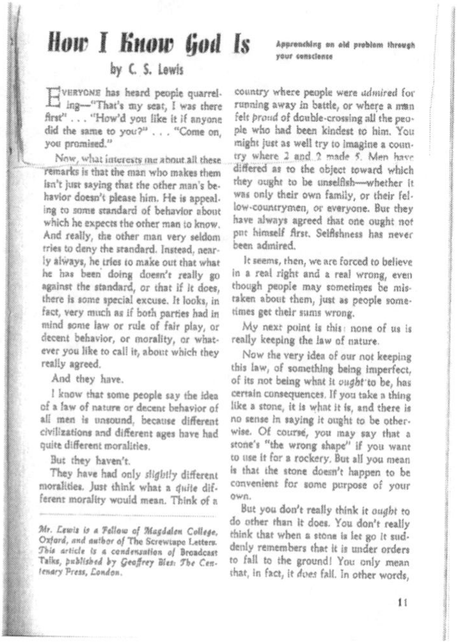

How I Know God Is

Approaching an old problem through your conscience

by C. S. Lewis

EVERYONE has heard people quarreling—"That's my seat, I was there first" . . . "How'd you like it if anyone did the same to you?" . . . "Come on, you promised."

Now, what interests me about all these remarks is that the man who makes them isn't just saying that the other man's behavior doesn't please him. He is appealing to some standard of behavior about which he expects the other man to know. And really, the other man very seldom tries to deny the standard. Instead, nearly always, he tries to make out that what he has been doing doesn't really go against the standard, or that if it does, there is some special excuse. It looks, in fact, very much as if both parties had in mind some law or rule of fair play, or decent behavior, or morality, or whatever you like to call it, about which they really agreed.

And they have.

I know that some people say the idea of a law of nature or decent behavior of all men is unsound, because different civilizations and different ages have had quite different moralities.

But they haven't.

They have had only *slightly* different moralities. Just think what a *quite* different morality would mean. Think of a country where people were *admired* for running away in battle, or where a man felt *proud* of double-crossing all the people who had been kindest to him. You might just as well try to imagine a country where 2 and 2 made 5. Men have differed as to the object toward which they ought to be unselfish—whether it was only their own family, or their fellow-countrymen, or everyone. But they have always agreed that one ought not put himself first. Selfishness has never been admired.

It seems, then, we are forced to believe in a real right and a real wrong, even though people may sometimes be mistaken about them, just as people sometimes get their sums wrong.

My next point is this: none of us is really keeping the law of nature.

Now the very idea of our not keeping this law, of something being imperfect, of its not being what it *ought* to be, has certain consequences. If you take a thing like a stone, it is what it is, and there is no sense in saying it ought to be otherwise. Of course, you may say that a stone's "the wrong shape" if you want to use it for a rockery. But all you mean is that the stone doesn't happen to be convenient for some purpose of your own.

But you don't really think it *ought* to do other than it does. You don't really think that when a stone is let go it suddenly remembers that it is under orders to fall to the ground! You only mean that, in fact, it *does* fall. In other words,

Mr. Lewis is a Fellow of Magdalen College, Oxford, and author of The Screwtape Letters. *This article is a condensation of* Broadcast Talks, *published by Geoffrey Bles: The Centenary Press, London.*

11

Figure 3.5. Leaders of the InterVarsity Christian Fellowship, including the editors of its monthly *HIS* magazine, led American evangelicals in coming to appreciate Lewis. This excerpt in *HIS* from *The Case for Christianity* appeared in February 1944.

months *HIS* provided a late but highly appreciative review of *The Screwtape Letters.* Accompanying this review was a short bio that informed readers about Lewis's books of literary scholarship as well as his popular Christian writings. It ended with an unreserved recommendation: "Here is a man who, though until recently an atheist[,] has eyes that see clearly, a mind unbefogged, a heart attuned to the Saviour, and a sense of humor that can put anything across."[37]

[37]C. S. Lewis, "How I Know God Is," *HIS* (February 1944): 11-13; Waldo Richardson, "Why Does God Allow Crime, War, and Disease?," *HIS* (October 1945): 10-12, quotation 11 (review of *The Problem of Pain*); Virginia Lowell, review of *The Screwtape Letters, HIS* (January 1946): 21-22, quotation 21.

A year later, in 1947, Donald Grey Barnhouse, a well-known radio preacher and pastor of Philadelphia's Tenth Presbyterian Church, added glowing words about Lewis in *Revelation*, the magazine he edited to circulate his views. Barnhouse reported that he was being "frequently asked his opinion" about Lewis. His standard reply described Lewis as "part of a great campaign of witness on behalf of simple evangelical Christianity by a man who is born again but who is using unorthodox means to spread his orthodoxy." Barnhouse went on to say that Lewis was confounding "Liberals who have thought all along all Fundamentalists to be ignoramuses" and that "Christians who have contacts with university students and faculty members" should be giving them Lewis's books.[38]

Clearly, by 1947, the Lewis tide among fundamentalists and evangelicals was beginning to turn. The few who responded positively to Lewis were themselves harbingers of a new day. Perfunctory notices in *The Christian Herald* and the *Sunday School Times* indicated that Lewis was gaining a hearing in constituencies not otherwise attuned to imaginative or learned presentations of the faith or favorable to books written by nonfundamentalists. Elisabeth Elliot, the Wheaton College student who told her parents about Lewis, would soon write with increasing sensitivity about the problems as well as the triumphs of missionary service.[39] In so doing, she moved beyond the hagiography usually accorded missionaries in fundamentalist circles. When *HIS* magazine published its favorable notices of Lewis, it was being edited by Kenneth Taylor, who in not too many years would publish *The Living Letters* and then *The Living Bible* as an alternative translation to the King James Version, which had been universally favored by American fundamentalists.[40] As another indication of

---

[38]Donald Grey Barnhouse, *Revelation*, 1947; quoted here from "C. S. Lewis," *Religious Digest* (May 1947): 14.

[39]Elisabeth Elliot, *The Savage My Kinsmen* (Ann Arbor, MI: Servant, 1961); Elliot, *No Graven Image* (New York: Harper & Row, 1966).

[40]Andrew T. LePeau and Linda Doll, *Heart, Soul, Mind, Strength: An Anecdotal History of InterVarsity Press, 1947–2007* (Downers Grove, IL: InterVarsity Press, 2006), 42.

shifting tectonic plates, the positive review of Lewis's *Problem of Pain* was followed in *HIS* by an article from Canadian Margaret Clarkson explaining why crude methods of personal evangelism undermined the faith. As the author of "We Come, O Christ, to Thee," for the first InterVarsity (later Urbana) Missionary Conference, Clarkson testified to a new appreciation for poetry and the arts among readers poised to appreciate the same from Lewis.[41]

For his part, Donald Grey Barnhouse, with a strong dispensational theology, a propensity for describing current events as the fulfillment of biblical prophecy, and a confrontational preaching style, could be considered a typical fundamentalist. But the years this Presbyterian spent leading a weekly Bible study at a New York City Lutheran church, his loyalty to the main northern Presbyterian denomination when other conservatives broke away, and his willingness to criticize fellow conservatives as sharply as he did theological liberals revealed that Barnhouse was also, in Joel Carpenter's conclusion, "a leader of the new evangelical movement."[42]

In other words, the reputation of C. S. Lewis among evangelicals, even in these years when they lagged behind Catholics and the secular media in engaging Lewis's books, showed that change was in the air. Appreciation for what Lewis did well, rather than worries about the exact shape of his theology or about his lack of evangelical credentials, would soon become the overwhelmingly dominant story among an ever-increasing number of Lewis's appreciative evangelical readers.

---

[41]Margaret Clarkson, "How Not to Witness," *HIS* (October 1945): 13-14. "We Come, O Christ, to You," *Psalter Hymnal Handbook*, ed. Emily R. Brink and Bert Pohlman (Grand Rapids, MI: CRC, 1998), 375-76.

[42]Joel A. Carpenter, "Barnhouse, Donald Grey," in *Dictionary of Christianity in America*, ed. Daniel G. Reid, Robert D. Linder, Bruce L. Shelley, and Harry Stout (Downers Grove, IL: InterVarsity Press, 1990), 117-18.

AMERICAN PROTESTANTISM IN THE 1940s

Protestant responses to C. S. Lewis in these earlier years reveal at least two important matters about the nation's Protestant population—one self-evident, the other not so obvious. The self-evident matter was the pivotal role Lewis played for individuals and groups deliberately turning aside from fundamentalism to embrace what they regarded as a fuller, more satisfying, and more authentically evangelical Christian faith. For the neo-evangelical generation, led by national figures such as Carl Henry, E. J. Carnell, Henrietta Mears, and Billy Graham, C. S. Lewis demonstrated that orthodox Christianity could be fully compatible with advanced learning, literary creativity, frank psychological insight, and even wit. For Clyde Kilby and then a host of others in Christian higher education, Lewis provided the same inspiration as they sought a better way to join faith, life, and learning. The ongoing programs of the Wade Center are only one of countless examples in the contemporary evangelical world reaffirming what Elisabeth Howard wrote when she said, "You all should read . . . his works."

The not-so-obvious matter from the 1940s is that the American Protestant world contained a much stronger *center* than standard accounts of division between fundamentalists and modernists, between liberals and conservatives, or between evangelicals and nonevangelicals suggest. In the years we are considering, fundamentalists on the way to becoming evangelicals were joined by a host of mainline Episcopalians, Lutherans, Presbyterians, Methodists, Southern Baptists, and more who, whatever their differences, agreed on the merits of what C. S. Lewis was writing. This common appreciation stretched from those who were conservative but not far right to those who were mainline but not far left. The commonality indicated that Lewis's way of presenting "mere Christianity" through careful scholarship, creative imagination, and compelling prose spoke to a large portion of the American Protestant world.

Responses to Lewis in the 1940s certainly undercut assumptions that took for granted a bifurcated Protestant world of two antagonistic parties. That historical lesson is one worth relearning today in a world where intra-Christian differences mean even less than a generation or two ago. The reception of C. S. Lewis resounds as an example of what might happen if believers chose to maximize what they shared and accorded differences a lower place in their ranking of priorities.

AND TODAY?

At the end of three chapters describing what C. S. Lewis's American readers appreciated as the first wave of his books became available in the United States, it is appropriate to think briefly about those years in relation to our situation today. On the one hand, it is fairly easy to describe the qualities that made Lewis a phenomenon in America even before the Narnia tales and *Mere Christianity* propelled him to the uniquely popular status he continues to enjoy in many, though of course not all, parts of the world. On the other hand, it is more difficult to spell out how circumstances that have changed since the 1940s affect the credible presentation of orthodox Christian faith in our own day.

To answer the question about what Americans valued in Lewis's works is tantamount to specifying characteristics that ensure writing about Christianity remains faithful to the nature of Christianity itself and that makes such writing effective. In a simplified summary, Americans saw Lewis as *deeply learned, theologically focused,* and *unusually creative.* Implicitly, they also recognized that his articulation of the faith was savvy and courageous.

First, he was *deeply learned.* For Americans prone to regard Oxford and Cambridge as sites of unusual intellectual depth, Lewis's connections, first to Oxford and then to Cambridge, gave his writing a distinctive Oxbridge cachet. But especially the Catholic critics, along with the Protestant Chad Walsh, who were learned people themselves, recognized that a great strength of Lewis's popular writing was the extensive reservoir of literary knowledge he brought to his popular works. By exploiting the riches of classical Western literature, Lewis demonstrated that variations on older themes, when presented creatively, could capture the attention of modern readers. Those critics also saw that Lewis did not flaunt his extraordinary learning; he was never pretentious. Also importantly, he did not treat his own learning instrumentally—that is, Lewis did not immerse himself in the literary past in order to fashion a weapon for Christian apologetics. The scholarship was rather an organic part of his person that flowed naturally into his imaginative and apologetical writing.

And today? Deep, thorough, and wide-ranging learning in a believer's chosen field will guarantee that the believer's writing has depth, integrity, and solidity, which are the most important things—whatever the public reception.

Second, Lewis was *theologically focused.* The entire body of his work demonstrated the wisdom of emphasizing what the main Christian traditions held in common, instead of advocating only one of Christianity's many competing varieties. For Roman Catholics, Lewis paid too little attention to the church. Fundamentalists worried that he did not emphasize their fundamentals. Reformed evangelicals thought he was deficient in philosophy. To mainline Protestants he could seem quaint or old-fashioned. To the mainstream media he was a curiosity for his eagerness to defend traditional Christianity. But because Lewis's presentation of traditional Christianity was so winsome, thought-provoking, and (again) creative, he gained an appreciative audience among all these groups for Christianity defined in basic traditional terms.

Today, there is no guarantee that writing oriented toward "mere Christianity" will gain a hearing. It is, however, almost certain that writing advocating only one variety of Christianity will *not* gain a wide public hearing.

Third, Lewis's *unusual creativity* may simply be a quality that cannot be caught, taught, or replicated. A remarkable centennial tribute by J. I. Packer—a Reformed, evangelical, Low-Church Anglican who believed in biblical inerrancy—for Lewis, a non-Reformed, non-evangelical, High-Church Anglican who did not believe in biblical inerrancy, described Lewis's genius perceptively. The "secret" of his "great piercing power," according to Packer, lay in Lewis's "blend of logic and imagination. . . . All of his arguments (including his literary criticism) are illustrations, in the sense they throw light directly on realities of life and action, while all his illustrations (including the fiction and fantasies) are arguments, in the sense that they throw light directly on realities of truth and fact."[43]

Today, the Christian world benefits from quite a few believers writing for the public who are learned and who are focused on the main Christian traditions, but few if any manifest the qualities that made Lewis, in the strict sense of the word, unique. Since efforts to *imitate* Lewis always fall short and usually seem forced, the wisest course is to cultivate whatever gifts a believer enjoys with whatever skill the believer possesses and then not to worry about measuring the outcome against the gifts that Lewis enjoyed so richly and cultivated so well.

If Lewis's creativity was unique, the savvy he displayed can certainly be imitated. That savvy was most obvious in the indirection of his imaginative works and the humility of his straightforward Christian writing. In *Screwtape*, the Ransom Trilogy, *The Great Divorce*, and later the Narnia tales, Lewis gave shape to the organic Christianity of his being by addressing specific Christian matters indirectly. This skillful indirection worked powerfully, allowing him to

---

[43]J. I. Packer, "Still Surprised by Lewis," *Christianity Today*, September 7, 1998, 57.

say what he wanted to say in forms appropriate to the saying. In the directly Christian works, Lewis tried to persuade through the force of his arguments, presented with as much humor and psychological insight as possible. Maybe *unassuming* is a better word than *humble* for these efforts. Whatever it is called, Lewis's savvy about the modes of his expression holds up an example worthy of imitation.

Finally, Lewis displayed unusual courage in his writing. As Chad Walsh in the 1940s and Stephanie Derrick more recently have shown, Lewis was not afraid to appear unfashionable, plebian, or unprofessional to his Oxford University peers or to his era's guardians of advanced opinion. An apostle to the skeptics is bound to offend some of the skeptics, which did not seem to bother Lewis in the slightest. (Lewis did, however, take seriously criticism from his own small circle of friends.) He thus shows that trying to express what we know to be true, hopefully while enjoying a small circle of sympathetic friends whose critiques we trust, is more important than trying to impress whatever gatekeepers police the higher reaches of our particular fields.

The second question about the change of circumstances between Lewis's day and our own is complicated. In his fine study of Lewis, along with T. S. Eliot, Jacques Maritain, W. H. Auden, and Simone Weil, during the war years, Alan Jacobs describes clearly the situation in which these Christian intellectuals did their work:

> This was a time—it seems so long ago now, a very different age, and one that is unlikely to return—when prominent Christian thinkers in the West believed that they had a responsibility to set a direction not just for the churches but for the whole of society. And, stranger still, in that time, many of their fellow citizens were willing to grant them that authority.[44]

---

[44]Alan Jacobs, *The Year of Our Lord, 1943: Christian Humanism in an Age of Crisis* (New York: Oxford University Press, 2018), xi.

George Marsden, writing specifically about the United States' leading arbiters of culture in the early 1950s, offers a similar account of the cultural changes with which we live today: what these arbiters could not see

> was how near they were to the end of an era. The United States had been shaped by an alliance between enlightenment rationality and Protestant religion. . . . That arrangement still seemed to be flourishing throughout the 1950s. . . . Yet two decades later, after the cultural upheaval of the 1960s, the idea of a mainline Protestant establishment was hardly more than a memory.[45]

Today the public sphere, and not only in the United States, is at once more secular, more fragmented, and more focused on the here and now than what Jacobs and Marsden describe in their perceptive histories. It has become more secular for reasons identified authoritatively by figures such as David Martin, Alasdair MacIntyre, and Charles Taylor.[46] One result is that the West's residual Christian culture, exploited so fruitfully by Lewis—but also by Dorothy L. Sayers, T. S. Eliot, Chad Walsh, Charles Brady, and others—has slipped further away from general consciousness. Another result is that very little of the predisposition remains to think that guidance for all of society should come from practicing Christians. In fact, more of the public in the twenty-first century now believes that Christian communities are the least likely source from which to expect guidance for the whole of society.

The contemporary world has also become more intellectually fragmented, especially by social media that provide a public platform for

---

[45]George M. Marsden, *The Twilight of the American Enlightenment: The 1950s and the Crisis of Liberal Belief* (New York: Basic, 2014), 123.

[46]David Martin, *A General Theory of Secularization* (New York: Harper & Row, 1978); Alasdair MacIntyre, *After Virtue: A Study in Moral Theory* (Notre Dame, IN: Notre Dame University Press, 1981): Charles Taylor, *The Sources of the Self: The Making of the Modern Identity* (Cambridge, MA: Harvard University Press, 1989).

anyone with a functioning device who can attract the attention of an audience. Whatever the attraction, however bizarre or irresponsible, the fallout from democratized media accessibility has shaped the thinking of millions, even hundreds of millions. At the same time, the mesmerizing power of brilliantly engineered media has concentrated attention on what can be communicated impressionistically and immediately. In this frenetic cultural landscape, discursive logic, linear reasoning, respect for the past, images evoking rather than spelling out, and the willingness to test claims about matters of fact all suffer.

In such a world, Lewis's appeal to reasoned consideration of human nature or his imaginative articulation of Christian realities through indirect means can certainly continue to persuade—in fact, as indicated by the ongoing popularity of especially *Mere Christianity* and the Narnia tales, to persuade ever greater numbers in ever more parts of the world. Despite Cassandra-like tales of woe about the state of Christian cultural life, to which I have also contributed, we witness today a remarkable range of well-grounded, reasonably well-received, and persuasive Christian literary and intellectual efforts. Moreover, these efforts come from a great variety of Christian traditions and individuals representing those various traditions.

Such ones are replicating what, on a different scale, Lewis's American readers in the 1940s so manifestly appreciated. Between then and now, however, there exists a substantial gap. Appreciation among multitudes on the ground who value what Lewis exemplified does not translate up into a coherent force reframing general attitudes in the public sphere. It is not that these efforts are inherently defective but rather that the public sphere of the 1940s no longer exists and that the number of insistent voices demanding public attention has become so loud, so unforgiving, and so clamorous.

In these circumstances Lewis's attitude toward his own work may offer clearer guidance for Christian communicators than any particular product of his fruitful pen. In July 1942, *The Screwtape Letters* was a British sensation, Lewis was inundated with urgent queries from listeners to his first set of broadcast talks, and he had only just finished a complete draft of *Perelandra*. At that moment, at a high point of public visibility, he wrote a revealing letter to his close friend Sister Penelope, CSMV. In response to her inquiry about how she could pray for him, Lewis responded with a poem, "Apologist's Evening Hymn," which, he said, "I've just completed." It begins,

> From all my lame defeats and oh! much more
> From all the victories I have seemed to score;
> From cleverness shot forth in Thy behalf,
> At which, while angels weep, the audience laugh;
> From all my proofs of Thy divinity,
> Thou, who woulds't give no sign, deliver me.[47]

C. S. Lewis took great care in preparing his writings for the public. He certainly knew that many readers and listeners found them arrestingly illuminating, gratifyingly helpful, and singularly life-giving. Yet as he wrote to Sister Penelope, he seemed most concerned not with the success of the writings but with the soul of the writer. All who in our different circumstances aspire to speak, write, and publish for the cause of Christ and his kingdom would do well to follow *that* example.

---

[47]C. S. Lewis to Sister Penelope, CSMV, July 29, 1942, in *Books, Broadcasts, and the War, 1931–1949*, vol. 2 of *The Collected Letters of C. S. Lewis*, ed. Walter Hooper (San Francisco: HarperSanFrancisco, 2004), 527. This poem was later published with minor revisions as "The Apologist's Evening Prayer" in C. S. Lewis, *Poems*, ed. Walter Hooper (London: Geoffrey Bles, 1964).

RESPONSE

AMY E. BLACK

I APPRECIATE THE OPPORTUNITY to offer a few reflections on Mark Noll's insightful analysis. As usual, Noll has taken a seemingly straightforward task—in this case, analyzing the response of American Protestants to the work of C. S. Lewis—and offered significant new insights and questions to ponder.

I will focus my response on two central questions raised in Noll's analysis: (1) What is the goal of Christian communications? (2) What lessons can we learn from Lewis's writings and their reception that can help us be more effective communicators of the truths of Christianity?

Noll identifies two important conclusions from the Protestant response to Lewis. The first, what he calls a "self-evident matter," is indeed a natural takeaway from this history but one well worthy of our attention. Lewis's writings served as an important bridge between fundamentalism and neo-evangelicalism, charting a path theologically conservative Christians could follow toward meaningful cultural engagement.

Lewis was a learned scholar of English literature, but his body of work that reached so widely and is so central to his legacy is outside his narrow academic guild. We may not remember him so much for his academic works, but his classical training and intellectual pursuits enriched his writing, his attention to detail, and his depth of argument. A masterful storyteller, Lewis's fiction sheds new light on the gospel story and introduces biblical themes to wide audiences of all ages. In his apologetics and Christian nonfiction, he expounds biblical themes and expresses some genuinely contested theological views, but he never presents himself as a systematic theologian, nor does he seek to engage that particular academic audience. In both genres, he writes to lay Christians and those considering the faith, presenting Christianity to these more general audiences with the hope of pointing them to Christian truth.

In Noll's words, "C. S. Lewis demonstrated that orthodox Christianity could be fully compatible with advanced learning, literary creativity, frank psychological insight, and even wit." In their movement away from fundamentalism, neo-evangelicals needed models of excellence and faithful Christian writing, and Lewis offered this, demonstrating that works created for broader audiences could indeed bear much good fruit. Both Lewis's fiction and Christian non-fiction offer inspiring examples of using one's intellectual gifts for the furthering of God's kingdom.

Noll's second conclusion is equally instructive. His account of the various Protestant responses to Lewis unveils a common thread. Although Lewis of course had his critics, Noll's analysis reveals a widespread appreciation of Lewis that spans a surprisingly broad range of the theological spectrum. Critics on the far left and far right tended to be more dismissive, but Lewis spoke to—and continues to speak to—Christians from a range of backgrounds and theological locations. Much of the historical analysis of twentieth-century Protestantism focuses on its divisions, undoubtedly a significant theme, but such narratives often give too little attention to the many areas of agreement and collaboration among Protestants. The wide-ranging appreciation of Lewis's body of work reminds us that Christian communicators—with the right gifts and talents—can speak with a voice that resonates across a range of theological differences. Simply put, Lewis used his extraordinary gifts and talents to the glory of God, and we should seek to do likewise.

Popular Christian writing reveals an unavoidable tension between reaching new and broad audiences with the Christian message and writing with technical theological precision. Theological critiques are important; they clearly have their place in scholarly writing and serve the church and its leaders. But as was the case in some of the evangelical responses to Lewis, the critics' expectation of theological precision at times risked missing the forest for the trees. It is indeed fair to raise some doctrinal concerns, but it is also important to celebrate the broad reach of his works far outside academic circles and the opportunity this opens for introducing people to Christian ideas.

Noll's review of Protestant responses to Lewis ends on a cautionary note, and one that Christians need to consider thoughtfully. Dramatic cultural changes and the modern information age create challenges far different from the world Lewis inhabited. We need to be aware of these changes and try to respond to them as we seek to be effective communicators.

First, far fewer Americans are rooted in Christian culture now than when Lewis was writing, and the religious landscape of the United States is changing dramatically and quickly. The number of Christians is decreasing, and secularism is on the rise. Gallup polls in the 1950s recorded that more than nine of ten Americans said they were Christian.[1] According to a recent Pew Center survey, only 63 percent of Americans now identify as Christians. About 6 percent identify with other religions, and 29 percent are religiously unaffiliated.[2] In 1965, 70 percent of Americans said that "religion is very important in their life"; by 2021, only 41 percent shared that view.[3]

---

[1] Frank Newport, "Percentage of Christians in U.S. Drifting Down, but Still High," Gallup, December 24, 2015, https://news.gallup.com/poll/187955/percentage-christians-drifting-down-high.aspx.

[2] Gregory A. Smith, "In U.S., Roughly Three-in-Ten Adults Now Religiously Unaffiliated," Pew Research Center, December 14, 2021, www.pewresearch.org/religion/2021/12/14/about-three-in-ten-u-s-adults-are-now-religiously-unaffiliated/.

[3] Smith, "In U.S., Roughly Three-in-Ten Adults."

These dramatic shifts in religious allegiance create challenge and opportunity for Christian communication. For a report released in 2020, Michael Wear and I interviewed more than fifty Christian leaders and asked them about their work and witness in the face of increasing religious pluralism. The leaders we interviewed all acknowledged the growing religious pluralism of the United States. They expressed concern about increased division, but they also pointed to new opportunities for Christian action and witness. We found widespread agreement that Christianity offers distinct tools and perspectives to help bridge societal divides. As we summarized, "Christians share a moral language and vocabulary, even across denomination and political and theological perspectives, that provides a foundation for working together."[4] In other words, many Christian leaders today want to follow a path like the one Lewis charted before them.

Noll also offers a warning that today's public sphere is "intellectually fragmented" and dominated by "insistent voices." Indeed, the contemporary media environment is far different from that in Lewis's day, and it creates significant obstacles for effective Christian communication.

The rapid and vast expansion of news outlets and social media platforms has moved us from an era of broadcasting—messages designed for a wide audience—to one of narrowcasting—messages tailored to niche markets. The modern media age not only offers access to news and current events twenty-four hours a day, seven days a week, it also provides seemingly limitless outlets from which to choose. The range of choices makes it far too easy for people to self-select only those media sources that align with their existing ideological perspectives and beliefs. In such an environment, many media outlets become echo chambers. Facts are contested. Emotional appeals eclipse reason.

---

[4]Michael Wear and Amy E. Black, *Christianity, Pluralism, and Public Life in the United States: Insights from Christian Leaders* (Washington, DC: Trinity Forum, 2020), 5.

Social scientists have demonstrated many powerful and destructive results of this fragmented media landscape. Public trust has declined sharply, hostility to those who hold differing views has grown exponentially, and prior beliefs and biases create vast misperceptions. An end result of all these trends is that people are growing more alienated from those who hold differing views and are less willing or able to treat those who differ from them with dignity and respect.

Those seeking to share Christian truths will face many obstacles in this contested and emotionally charged public square, likely even more obstacles than Lewis faced in his day. We need bridge builders, people who have the gifts to communicate across divides and bring people together. Like Lewis, we need to find creative and distinctive ways to share Christianity that connect across traditions and perspectives.

The popularity and resonance of Lewis's work should inspire us. Even in our increasingly pluralistic and secular society, which looks far different from his time, Lewis points Christians to ways they might still have a meaningful voice. Gifted writers and artists can use their creative talents to introduce people to Christ and his upside-down kingdom in a range of genres and artistic outlets, even if at times they must leave the more complex biblical and theological debates to the biblical scholars, theologians, and their guilds.

It is fitting to have this conversation at Wheaton College, a liberal arts college committed to integrating authentic faith with learning across a broad range of academic disciplines. Lewis built on his academic training and communicated the gospel creatively and winsomely through his novels; others can communicate Christian truths through visual arts, musical compositions and performances, mathematical equations, historical analyses, and more. Few of us will have the genius Lewis displayed, nor will we achieve his level of renown, but that should not hinder us from seeking creative ways to use our talents and expertise to communicate God's truth.

CHARLES BRADY'S TWO ARTICLES FROM *AMERICA* ON C. S. LEWIS IN 1944

CHAPTER ONE EXPLAINS in detail the importance of early reviews of C. S. Lewis's works by American Catholic authors. As noted, among those reviews—or reviews by anyone else—none were as thorough, perceptive, and well-versed in literary history as the paired studies published in the spring of 1944 by Charles Brady. As also noted, Lewis himself thanked Brady as "the first of my critics so far who has really read and understood *all* of my books and 'made up' the subject in a way that makes you an authority."[1] Beyond the information provided in that chapter about this Canisius College English professor, it is noteworthy that he later reviewed several other works by Lewis, as well as by Charles Williams, J. R. R. Tolkien, and Dorothy Sayers. In the early 1960s Brady also planned to transform a lecture series on Lewis, Tolkien, and Sayers into a book he called at different stages of its preparation *Reclaim Imagination* or *The Oxford Magicians*. Yet after Brady negotiated with several publishers, including Sheed

---

[1] C. S. Lewis to Charles A. Brady, October 29, 1944, in *Books, Broadcasts, and the War, 1931–1949*, vol. 2 of *The Collected Letters of C. S. Lewis*, ed. Walter Hooper (San Francisco: HarperSanFrancisco, 2004), 629-31, quotation 629.

& Ward, which had published Lewis's *Pilgrim's Regress*, the project fell through. An anticipated subvention did not become available, and Brady also reported later that in those years "burgeoning creative output [his novels and stories] took precedence over the critical."[2] The learned quality of the articles that follow suggest that the book Brady did not complete might have become a very good book indeed.

The two articles are reprinted here with the permission of *America* magazine.

"INTRODUCTION TO LEWIS," *AMERICA* LXXI (MAY 27, 1944): 213-14.

I know someone will ask me, "Do you really mean, at this time of day, to re-introduce our old friend the devil—hoofs and horns and all?" Well, what the time of day has to do with it, I don't know. And I'm not particular about the hoofs and horns. But in other respects my answer is, "Yes, I do."

FROM *THE CASE FOR CHRISTIANITY*.

NOT many writers nowadays are on such terms of cordial insult with His Infernal Majesty as the ready Ulster-born professor of English literature at Oxford University, Mr. Clive Staples Lewis, has shown himself to be in what is by now the most phenomenally popular household book of applied religion of the twentieth century, *The Screwtape Letters*. Not since another Oxford don chose to divest himself of his academic robes and slip down a rabbit-hole with Alice in the White Rabbit has the reading world been given such a divertissement by a race of spectacled savants. Their share, you see, in providing human delight has been limited, in the main, to the Attic salt of old Benjamin Jowett, or obversely, to the pantomime

---

[2]Email from Kathleen DeLaney, Canisius College archivist, to Wade Center intern Elise Peterson, March 21, 2023.

role of satirical butt, as in Beerbohm's *Zuleika*, Dobson, Bellon's *Lines on a Don*, or Michael Innes' and Dorothy Sayers' university detective-story extravaganzas.

Let Dons Delight is Ronald Knox's pleasant motto for the port-wine chuckling mirth that reigns behind the sported oak, as philological puns drop like bright seed pearls from magistral lips and trout flies are prepared against the long summer recess. But then, to paraphrase Stern, sometimes they order these matters better in England; take Tolkien and Chambers, for example. And here is a don to delight the gods—the Olympian ones at least, if not those of Tartarus.

For, as in the case of the Curé d'Ars and his good friend *le vieux Grappin*, whatever condescending affection Mr. Lewis may feel for the Guy Fawkes target of his witty cocoanut shy, old Screwtape cannot

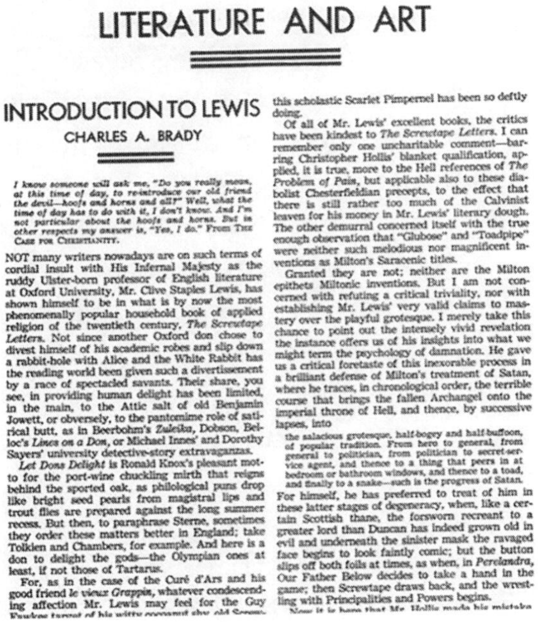

LITERATURE AND ART

INTRODUCTION TO LEWIS
CHARLES A. BRADY

I know someone will ask me, "Do you really mean, at this time of day, to reintroduce our old friend the devil—hoofs and horns and all?" Well, what the time of day has to do with it, I don't know. And I'm not particular about the hoofs and horns. But in other respects my answer is, "Yes, I do." From THE CASE FOR CHRISTIANITY.

NOT many writers nowadays are on such terms of cordial insult with His Infernal Majesty as the ruddy Ulster-born professor of English literature at Oxford University, Mr. Clive Staples Lewis, has shown himself to be in what is by now the most phenomenally popular household book of applied religion of the twentieth century, *The Screwtape Letters*. Not since another Oxford don chose to divest himself of his academic robes and slip down a rabbit-hole with Alice and the White Rabbit has the reading world been given such a divertissement by a race of spectacled savants. Their share, you see, in providing human delight has been limited, in the main, to the pantomime role of satirical butt, as in Beerbohm's *Zuleika*, Dobson, Belloc's *Lines on a Don*, or Michael Innes' and Dorothy Sayers' university detective-story extravaganzas.

Let Dons Delight is Ronald Knox's pleasant motto for the port-wine chuckling mirth that reigns behind the sported oak, as philological puns drop like bright pearls from magistral lips and trout flies are prepared against the long summer recess. But then, to paraphrase Sterne, sometimes they order these matters better in England; take Tolkien and Chambers, for example. And here is a don to delight the gods—the Olympian ones at least, if not those of Tartarus.

For, as in the case of the Curé d'Ars and his good friend *le vieux Grappin*, whatever condescending affection Mr. Lewis may feel for the Guy Fawkes target of his witty cocoanut shy, old Screwtape

this scholastic Scarlet Pimpernel has been so deftly doing.

Of all of Mr. Lewis' excellent books, the critics have been kindest to *The Screwtape Letters*. I can remember only one uncharitable comment—barring Christopher Hollis' blanket qualification, applied, it is true, more to the Hell references of *The Problem of Pain*, but applicable also to these diabolist Chesterfieldian precepts, to the effect that there is still rather too much of the Calvinist leaven for his money in Mr. Lewis' literary dough. The other demurral concerned itself with the true enough observation that "Glubose" and "Toadpipe" were neither such melodious nor magnificent inventions as Milton's Saracenic titles.

Granted they are not; neither are the Milton epithets Miltonic inventions. But I am not concerned with refuting a critical triviality, nor with establishing Mr. Lewis' very valid claims to mastery over the playful grotesque. I merely take this chance to point out the intensely vivid revelation the instance offers us of his insights into what we might term the psychology of damnation. He gave us a critical foretaste of this inexorable process in a brilliant defense of Milton's treatment of Satan, where he traces, in chronological order, the terrible course that brings the fallen Archangel onto the imperial throne of Hell, and thence, by successive lapses, into

the salacious grotesque, half-hoofy and half-buffoon, of popular tradition. From here to general, from general to politician, from politician to secret-service agent, and thence to a thing that peers in at bedroom or bathroom windows, and thence to a toad, and finally to a snake—such is the progress of Satan. For himself, he has preferred to treat of him in these latter stages of degeneracy, when, like a certain Scottish thane, the forsworn recreant to a greater lord than Duncan has indeed grown old in evil and underneath the sinister mask the ravaged face begins to look faintly comic; but the button slips off both foils at times, as when, in *Perelandra*, Our Father Below decides to take a hand in the game; then Screwtape draws back, and the wrestling with Principalities and Powers begins.

Now it is here that Mr. Hollis made his mistake

Figure A.1. The straightforward, no-nonsense typography of the American Jesuits' *America* magazine provided an ideal vehicle for Charles Brady's pathbreaking assessment of C. S. Lewis and his books.

be very kindly intentioned towards this quiet professor who finds so much fun in the Vanity Fair of Hell. For one thing, Cheapjack Scratch was getting away only too nicely with his various polite incognita, until this Nosy Parker had to come along to queer the pitch; for another, the Prince of Darkness, who was once a great gentleman whatever his present status as familiar of newt and eft, does not like to be laughed at; nor as a bureaucrat, does he care for any wiretapping in Tophet or embarrassing interference with the diplomatic mail-pouches of Eblis, both of which this scholastic Scarlet Pimpernel has been so deftly doing.

Of all Mr. Lewis' excellent books, the critics have been kindest to *The Screwtape Letters*. I can remember only one uncharitable comment—barring Christopher Hollis' blanket qualification, applied, it is true, more to the Hell references of *The Problem of Pain*, but applicable also to these diabolist Chesterfieldian precepts, to the effect that there is still rather too much of the Calvinist leaven for his money in Mr. Lewis' literary dough. The other demurral concerned itself with the true enough observation that "Glubose" and "Toadpipe" were neither such melodious nor magnificent inventions as Milton's Saracenic titles.

Granted they are not; neither are the Milton epithets Miltonic inventions. But I am not concerned with refuting a critical triviality, nor with establishing Mr. Lewis' very valid claims to mastery over the playful grotesque. I merely take this chance to point out the intensely vivid revelation the instance offers us of his insights into what we might term the psychology of damnation. He gave us a critical foretaste of this inexorable process in a brilliant defense of Milton's treatment of Satan, where he traces, in chronological order, the terrible course that brings the fallen Archangel onto the imperial throne of Hell, and thence, by successive lapses, into

the salacious grotesque, half-bogey and half-buffoon, of popular tradition. From hero to general, from general to politician, from politician to secret-service agent, and thence to a thing that peers in a bedroom or bathroom windows, and thence to a toad, and finally to a snake—such is the progress of Satan.

For himself, he has preferred to treat of him in these latter stages of degeneracy, when like a certain Scottish thane, the forsworn recreant to a greater lord than Duncan has indeed grown old in evil and underneath the sinister mask the ravaged face begins to look faintly comic; but the button slips off both foils at times, as when, in *Perelandra*, Our Father Below decides to take a hand in the game; then Screwtape draws back, and the wrestling with Principalities and Powers begins.

Now it is here that Mr. Hollis made him his mistake, forgetting, perhaps, that when John left Puritania in Mr. Lewis' spiritual autobiography, *The Pilgrim's Regress*, he left John Calvin behind forever—more irrevocably, in fact, than many Catholic Irishmen manage to do; and the book then carries us to a *Paradiso* as well as to an *Inferno*. Mr. Lewis' fantasy or, if you prefer, vision of Paradise, here and in *The Problem of Pain*, is, in one fashion, like the Irish myth of Tir-n-an-Og, the Land of Youth and, in another, like some Platonic archetype of English hearth and nursery, a blend, almost, of Sunday's house in *The Man Who Was Thursday* and Barrie's nursery under the nightlights, where dog Nana keeps guard over the sleeping children.

But the point I wish to make against Mr. Hollis is this: Mr. Lewis' teleology does not invoke the dour Calvinistic dogma of "you can't take it with you" but rather the exactly opposite doctrine of that sweet Scottish mystic, George MacDonald, his and Chesterton's "owne maister deere," who used to preach in sermon, poem and fantastic novel that you really can take it with you in the last analysis—all that counts, anyway, wife and child and candlelight and old cat purring on the hearth; toy theater and tavern; for man will remain man.

No one grudges Macmillan *Screwtape's* gratifying climb to best-sellerhood; it would be regrettable, however, if the reader should stop short here, or even if he went no further than *Out of the Silent Planet*, *Perelandra*, and *The Pilgrim's Regress*. For Mr. Lewis makes two other major demands upon our attention, the first of which, I am sure, needs no belaboring. He is the only truly popular champion of Orthodoxy—*The New Republic's* Alistair Cooke refers to "the alarming vogue of Mr. C.S. Lewis"—in book, pamphlet and radio address since the passing of Gilbert Keith Chesterton. Like Chesterton, he has no pretensions in the direction of theological authority; but for that very reason navies from the docks of Liverpool and fishermen in Lancashire pubs laugh appreciatively over a lecture on sexual ethics that illustrates the essential perversity of the strip-tease by suggesting that we do not alternatively titillate, then frustrate the appetite of hunger with Kleig lights trained on a coyly frying pork-chop which, at the moment of brown completion, is suddenly cloaked by darkness and a stage curtain to the admiring accompaniment of hoarse cheers.

But it would be a shame if his critical work and scholarly essays were confined to the lamp-lit circle of those dull persons who subscribe to *English Studies* and *Modern Language Notes*. Mr. Lewis' veins run blood, not ink; there is no mildew in his bones; nor mere jargon on his lips.

He has to his credit in *The Allegory of Love*, which won the Hawthornden award for 1936, the best critical treatment in English of Chaucer's psychological romance, *Troilus and Criseyde*; the finest book of general commentary I know of on *Paradise Lost* in *A Preface to Paradise Lost*; and, I will go bond, the most superb single essay consideration of the sweet Prince of Elsinore in *Hamlet: The Prince or the Poem*, the annual Shakespeare lecture of the British Academy for 1942. It is a formidable record; three great disquisitions on three of our literature's four Titans. A successful critique of Dickens would square the circle. That is a consummation devoutly to be hoped for, of course; in the meantime we have such fascinating miscellanea as his "Personalist" controversy with his friend, Dr. Tillyard, recorded in *The Personalist Heresy*; and *Rehabilitations*, a fine essay collection containing defenses of such disparate things and persons as Shelley, Morris, the Oxford English curriculum, Anglo-Saxon metrics, and *Peter Rabbit*.

Even the non-professional reader, who has but slight concern with matters of prosody and literary history, will find much to delight him in these pages; and no enthusiast of Lewis, English scholar or not, can afford to overlook the humane scholarship, as excellent in its respective fields as Ker's or Chambers' in theirs, of this very humanistic, and therefore Catholic, don.

It is true, however, that there are two lobes to the Lewis brain, both working at once to produce a more than three-dimensional stereo-scopic reality, but one coloring the field of vision more at one time, the other at another. This was also true of Chesterton, his great con-gener, in whom one could distinguish a rationalistic and a mystic lobe. In Lewis' instance both lobes turn at once on a pivot of wit; but there is a lobe of Swiftian fancy and a lobe of Dunsanyesque—the term is used to indicate kind, not degree—imagination, both crossing and criss-crossing and bewildering simultaneity, with Swift predomi-nating in *Screwtape* and the Tir-n-an-Og Dunsay in *Perelandra* and *Out of the Silent Planet*, where instead of Eighteenth Century efts and ouphs of fancy à la Voltaire or Alexander Pope we sight our crossbows for the great Albatross, the splendid Oyarsa of the imagination, who haunts the ringing crags of myth rather than the pleasant upland slopes of allegory.

This latter charming qualification applies to *The Pilgrim's Regress*, in which Lewis, who, as a scholar, has found himself in reaction against today's contemptuous depreciation of that old-fashioned form, seems to have set out to prove he could write as good allegory as Bunyan. The resultant, half-medieval, half seventeenth-century Puritan, reveals the Bedford Tinker's iron somewhat mitigated by the sweetly silver musical alloy of nursery rhyme, of *Boys and girls come out to play, The moon is shining bright as day.* Wisdom's wanton children gambol in the moonlight; the moon shines soft and clear on Mother Kirk's pool of Baptism; but it is still the familiar moon of earthly nurseries after the Fall. Malacandra and Perelandra gleam fair with the further radiance of Mars and Venus cleansed of the perilous stuff that Original Sin brought into our silent world, the pure planets of Chesterton's dream, freed of the incestuous associations of mortal legend.

Next time I shall allot adequate space and time to Mr. Lewis' two time-and-space fantasies for the very cogent reasons that I consider their Miltonic grandeur of conception the greatest exercise of pure imagination in immediately contemporary literature, and because, with a few notable exceptions, the nation's reviewers have treated these strange masterpieces very shabbily. This indictment includes the Catholic reviewers as well; feckless creatures that they are, they even missed the orthodox *Candide* in the book, *Out of the Silent Planet.*

That is another story and, perhaps, I grow indignant for small cause; there is a great presumption that no good can come out of Nazareth and, at first, *The Man Who Was Thursday* experienced a like sorry fate.

"C.S. LEWIS: II," *AMERICA* LXXI (JUNE 10, 1944): 269-70.

IT is instructive to note the form Mr. Lewis has chosen for his imaginative Pegasus; the blunt-nosed space-ship of Verne and Wells. It is instructive for two reasons. First, it provides an obvious revelation of his relish for the right recognized masterpieces in the *genre* from H.G. Wells' *Time Machine* to Edgar Rice Burroughs' *Martian* series. (Yes, Burroughs, too, literary *snobbistes*; even if he does not cite by name amid his popular predilections this American Dumas of Tarzana, California, there is a distinct probability, I should say, that the Lord and Lady of Perelandra owe their green color to his Tars Tarkas and Sola rather than to the more academically presentable *Gawain and the Green Knight.*)

More importantly, this choice of *genre* cast some light on one of his most firmly-held critical tenants: to wit that, nowadays, one of the crying needs of modern criticism is a "defense of the disinterested literary enjoyment in general against certain dangerous tendencies," against "that new Puritanism which has captured many critics and taught us to object to pleasure in poetry simply because it is pleasure." There is none of this false snobbery about a man who dares to reject *Ulysses,* who includes among his favorite books *She* and *Peter Rabbit,* and who is willing to hazard the guess in *Rehabilitations* that our age may be known to posterity "not as that of Eliot and Auden but as that of Buchan and Wodehouse (and stranger things have come to pass.)"

A too-constricting, indeed belittling significance, however, has been read into this employment of the inter-planetary travel fantasy. It is true that from the point of view of social criticism Mr. Lewis ranges himself with the anti-Utopianists—Huxley, Noyes and Benson—as against the Utopianists—Shaw and Wells; it is equally true that too much has been made of this point even by so sensitively percipient an appreciator of *Out of the Silent Planet* as Christopher Morley, when he describes Mr. Lewis' interest in his elected form as "ethical and philosophical rather than scientific"; which is true enough so far as it goes, though *theological* would have been a more searching epithet to apply.

No, the fact of the matter is, in these volumes, contrary to his urbane stance in *The Screwtape Letters,* he is not being primarily satirical. He is creating fantasy on an intensely imaginative plane of great beauty; and even where he indulges in parable, as in the strangely moving encounter between Ransom and the *hrossa*—which can be interpreted, if you wish, as an allegory of racial fear and repugnance and its sublimation into deep affection through the very recognition of the fact of difference—the general effect is that of queerly lovable myth of such universal validity that Jung might well describe it as an archetype.

It is blinding flashes of revelation such as the foregoing that make us realize Mr. Lewis' piercing power of psychological penetration on several simultaneous and unusual planes: that of the diabolical level, as in *Screwtape*; the angelic, as in *Perelandra*; and the human and non-human, as here in *Out of the Silent Planet*. One might almost describe him as being in emphatic *rapport* with Thrones and Dominions and, more dangerously, with the "black archon" and his fellow Cosmocrats of the Dark Aeon. But we digress. To revert to Wells again, Mr. Lewis is very much at odds with his stellar imperialism; he has shrugged off, contemptuously, the usual egotistical and geocentric white-man's-burden assumption of *Amazing Stories* that the planets are populated by sinister creatures of superhuman cunning but subhuman malignity; fit subjects for annihilation or exploitation as colonial serfs by the superior earthling.

In fact, he puts the boot on the other foot, and virtuous beings of undoubted rationality reflect sadly on our earth as the Bent Planet, a star deflected from normality—where Maleldil, the Supreme Being, is a prince exiled from enemy-occupied territory, and rule is held by an evil usurper over us, members of the spiritual underground. An even more instructive contrast would describe Mr. Lewis' work as the very fantasy of free will, as dolphin-sport with the prime *If* of history, while Shaw's and Wells' are ingenious speculation in futurities, on the unsound basis of a self-invented currency, on the basis of what will be, not, as in Mr. Lewis' orthodox assumption, on the basis of what might have been, if it had not been for the Primal Sin, or what may still be on stars under the suzerainty of some angelic mandate rather than the Luciferian Bent One.

His pages are a melodious sounding-board, a whispering-gallery haunted by the echoes of what is great in world literature from the *Aeneid* (which, he says, "I have read through more often than I have read any long poem") to R.H. Benson, Olaf Stapledon, Rider Haggard and Ronald Knox. His taste in dragons is expert like Tolkien's, an Oxford colleague's, who wrote *The Hobbit* and of whom he has written in Anglo-Saxon alliterative verse: *We were talking of dragons, Tolkien and I, in a Berkshire Bar.* His sense of landscape recalls the mountains of William Morris' romances, in whose regard he said once: "Other stories have only scenery; his have geography." The heath-stepper Grendel and his awful dam stare out at us through the eyes of the Un-Man, who crawls after Ransom with the hideous zombie automatism of some dead watcher in a saga barrow. Swift did no better in *Gulliver* than Lewis has done with *hrossa* and *pfifltriggi*: and the proud resonance of Ransom *hnakrapunt*, or Ransom nicor-slayer, is beyond the purely playful powers of his fellow Irishman. Newman would have welcomed the clean sublime of the *Eldila*; Chaucer, perhaps, have recognized his "air-ish beasts" in some of the creatures that inhabit Malacandra; "*sorn*-haunted forests" is as good as any of the weird inventions of Dunsay; and Rackham and Syme would have hugged themselves over the chance to picture the same gaunt goblins. And, most endearing of all the radiant influences that play in light upon this new genius in our literature, are the heraldic things suggestive of the medieval bestiaries, one of whom, this singing beast, has been singled out for ecstatic mention in Leonard Bacon's fine review for the *Saturday Review*.

But the great sources are Revelation, the Myths of the world, and Milton; and I am not so certain that the last-mentioned august figure, to whom, temperamentally, Mr. Lewis is so dissimilar, is still not the most important. His reliance on Revelation is sufficiently obvious to require no demonstration; he is borne up in life and letters by the great central facts of our Christian faith as Ransom was by the waves of Perelandra's warm-pulsing ocean. So far as regards myth, which becomes, increasingly, a major preoccupation of psychologists such as Jung, men of letters such as Joyce and Kafka, and students of comparative religion from Frazer to Jessie Weston, he has done for myth much what Chesterton earlier did for fairy-tales in a famous chapter of *Orthodoxy*.

Only he goes farther than G.K.C. when, with a certain appealing humility that disarms any possible charge of audacity, he has Ransom question, on first seeing Perelandra's tiny dragon and wee Garden of the Hesperides, as a little boy new to Malory's Avalon might question: "Were all the things which appeared as mythology on earth scattered through other worlds as realities?" Later he sees the celestial archetypes of Ares and Aphrodite, and the reader's mind recalls with quiet joy what G.K.C. had said of the good gods in *The Everlasting Man*, rather than Milton's harsh strictures on the pagan deities: "damned crew"; and one's soul leaps at the realization that Bishop Corbet may long since have taken heart in Paradise in the sure knowledge that *Arcades'* magic plaint was, after all, unnecessary, and that nymphs and shepherds need really weep no more.

But always it is to Milton that he and we return; to that uncongenial and majestic spirit of English letters. Lewis is a more religious man, certainly, but that is beside the point; just read his superb critique, *A Preface to Paradise Lost*, as a preface to *Perelandra* and *Out of the Silent Planet*, and you will see for yourself what considerations of space preclude my indicating. I cannot refrain, however, in all due reverence, pointing out two instances where this modern poet of the angels surpasses his great master. First, the *eldila* talk in a way that satisfies our sense of artistic consistency and in a way that Milton's heavenly gourmand, Raphael, never attains. It is true, of course, as Newman reminds us, that men cannot comprehend the "experiences of angels"; but neither do we know how animals talk, if they do talk, and yet Kipling's *Jungle Book* translations from panther, python and bear are magnificently gratifying.

At any rate, whatever the merits of *eldila* conversation as authentic archangelese, Lewis succeeds where he charges *She* fails, in making his gravely noble invented diction suit the supernatural wisdom he imputes to his spiritual creatures. Second, he passes with flying Oxonian colors a test that Milton flunked: the representation of un-fallen sexuality without bringing in the perverse relish that accompanies human experience. "I can conceive of a successful treatment," he writes. "I believe that if Dante had chosen to paint such a thing, he might have succeeded." Elsewhere he calls Milton and Shelley the two halves of Dante, and we know what he means; that gloomy Saturnian amorous, "the lady of Christ's," lacked the requisite Shelleyan lightness. But Mr. Lewis is too modest. He need not go back so far in time as Dante. He has pulled it off himself in *Perelandra*, which might be called *Paradise Kept*.

There are other things I might have said at length. That Weston's transformation into the Un-Man is the most terrifying and con-vincing instance of diabolical possession in English letters since Benson's *Necromancers*; far more thoroughgoing, for example, than the Jekyll-and-Hyde ambivalence of Walpole's posthumorous *Killer and the Slain*. That he has a coolly classic perfection of epithet—for instance, Ransom's adventure produces in him an emotion of "severe delight"—and, again, referring to his new-found sense of Beauty in the Beast, he explains the *hrossa*'s strange appeal as "the shy, ineluc-table fascination of unlike for unlike." But time does not serve.

There is one final thing I cannot resist saying. Look at Francis O'Brien Garfield's sensitive wood-block of Clive Staples Lewis on the cover of the *Saturday Review* for April 8, 1944. The background is a zodiacal montage of what seems to be exploding *novae* and the ptero-dactyl figure of our old friend the Perelandrian dragon. It is a back-ground that fits some Druidic wizard precipitated out of the pleasant mists of the centuries that brood soft above the British Isles. Only the clean-shaven face of Mr. Lewis, citizen of Ulster and of Oxford, is that of a more recent ecclesiastical line than the Druids. One ought to leave such things to Strachey and Beerbohm but, somehow, it is the face of an English Bishop of Becket's or Wolsey's time. The reader may make what he will of these two divergent analogs. But I have a hunch, a hunch I do not have about Mr. Lewis' great good friend and co-religionist Mr. T.S. Eliot. I think Mr. Eliot is satisfied with the half-way house.

CONTRIBUTORS

Mark A. Noll (PhD, Vanderbilt University) is emeritus professor of history at Wheaton College and the University of Notre Dame. He is the author of many books, including *America's Book: The Rise and Decline of a Bible Civilization, 1794-1911, Jesus Christ and the Life of the Mind, Clouds of Witnesses: Christian Voices from Africa and Asia, The New Shape of World Christianity, The Rise of Evangelicalism: The Age of Edwards, Whitefield and the Wesleys, The Civil War as a Theological Crisis, Turning Points: Decisive Moments in the History of Christianity*, and *The Scandal of the Evangelical Mind*.

Karen J. Johnson (PhD, University of Illinois at Chicago) is associate professor of history at Wheaton College. Her expertise is the relationship between religion and race. She is the author of *One in Christ: Chicago Catholics and the Quest for Interracial Justice*.

Kirk D. Farney (PhD, University of Notre Dame) is vice president for advancement, vocation, and alumni engagement and a member of the history faculty at Wheaton College. He is the author of *Ministers of a New Medium: Broadcasting Theology in the Radio Ministries of Fulton J. Sheen and Walter A. Maier*.

Amy E. Black (PhD, Massachusetts Institute of Technology) is professor of political science at Wheaton College. She is the author or editor of several books, including *Honoring God in Red or Blue* and *Five Views on the Church and Politics*. Her work focuses on American political institutions and religion and politics.

IMAGE CREDITS

Figure I.1: Book cover of first American edition of *The Screwtape Letters*. Courtesy of Marion E. Wade Center, Wheaton College, IL. Used by permission.

Figure I.2: C. S. Lewis. Courtesy of Marion E. Wade Center, Wheaton College, IL. Used by permission.

Figure 1.1: Anne Fremantle, 1938 by Bassano Ltd: © National Portrait Gallery, London. Used by permission.

Figure 1.2: Charles A. Brady, 1949: Courtesy of Canisius College Archives and Special Collections, Scrapbook Collection of Charles A. Brady, Volume VI.

Figure 1.3: Thomas Merton. Used with Permission of the Merton Legacy Trust and the Thomas Merton Center at Bellarmine University.

Figure 1.4: Book cover of first American edition of *The Abolition of Man*. Courtesy of Marion E. Wade Center, Wheaton College, IL. Used by permission.

Figure 2.1: Arthur O. Lovejoy, photo by Greystone, NY, 1940: Special Collections, Sheridan Library, John Hopkins University. Every effort has been made to contact the photographer for permission to use this image.

Figure 2.2: W. H. Auden, photographer Howard Coster, 1937: © National Portrait Gallery, London. Used by permission.

Figure 2.3: Professor Chad Walsh, ca. 1945, Beloit College. Photograph: Courtesy of Beloit College Archives. Used by permission.

Figure 2.4: Book cover of first American edition of *Miracles*. Courtesy of Marion E. Wade Center, Wheaton College, IL. Used by permission.

Figure 3.1: *The Presbyterian Guardian*, June 22, 1936. Courtesy of the Committee on Christian Education, Orthodox Presbyterian Church. Used by permission.

Figure 3.2: Clyde S. Kilby, ca. 1935-36. Courtesy of Marion E. Wade Center, Wheaton College, IL. Used by permission.

Figure 3.3: *Moody Monthly*, December 1943. Used by permission of Moody Publishers.

Figure 3.4: Elizabeth Elliot, ca. 1940s-50s. Courtesy of Buswell Library Archives & Special Collections, Wheaton College, IL. Used by permission.

Figure 3.5: *HIS* Magazine, February 1944. Used by permission of InterVarsity Christian Fellowship/USA.

Figure A.1: We are grateful to *America* magazine for permission granted to reprint two articles from 1944 by Charles Brady.

NAME INDEX

SUBJECT INDEX

The Marion E. Wade Center

Founded in 1965, the Marion E. Wade Center of Wheaton College, Illinois, houses a major research collection of writings and related materials by and about seven British authors: Owen Barfield, G. K. Chesterton, C. S. Lewis, George MacDonald, Dorothy L. Sayers, J. R. R. Tolkien, and Charles Williams. The Wade Center collects, preserves, and makes these resources available to researchers and visitors through its reading room, museum displays, educational programming, and publications. All of these endeavors are a tribute to the importance of the literary, historical, and Christian heritage of these writers. Together, these seven authors form a school of thought, as they valued and promoted the life of the mind and the imagination. Through service to those who use its resources and by making known the words of its seven authors, the Wade Center strives to continue their legacy.

THE HANSEN LECTURESHIP SERIES

The Ken and Jean Hansen Lectureship is an annual lecture series named in honor of former Wheaton College trustee Ken Hansen and his wife, Jean, and endowed in their memory by Walter and Darlene Hansen. The series features three lectures per academic year by a Wheaton College faculty member on one or more of the Wade Center authors with responses by fellow faculty members.

Kenneth and Jean (née Hermann) Hansen are remembered for their welcoming home, deep appreciation for the imagination and the writings of the Wade authors, a commitment to serving others, and their strong Christian faith. After graduation from Wheaton College, Ken began working with Marion Wade in his residential cleaning business (later renamed ServiceMaster) in 1947. After Marion's death in 1973, Ken Hansen was instrumental in establishing the Marion E. Wade Collection at Wheaton College in honor of his friend and business colleague.